Book D
Teacher's Guide and Answer Key

VOCABULARY

FROM

CLASSICAL ROOTS®

Norma Fifer ▾ Nancy Flowers

EDUCATORS PUBLISHING SERVICE
Cambridge and Toronto

Editors: Stacey L. Nichols, Jen Noon

Managing Editor: Sheila Neylon

Printed in Eau Claire, WI, in April 2016

ISBN 978-0-8388-0863-4

7 8 9 10 DOC 19 18 17 16

Contents

Introduction

Words derived from Greek and Latin roots account for about 60 percent of the English language. By learning the most common roots and frequently used affixes, students can unlock the meanings of thousands of words. *Vocabulary from Classical Roots®* can help students learn these roots and prefixes so that they succeed not only with this series, but also with new words they encounter in daily life. The Teacher's Guide is a powerful educational tool that complements, extends, and enriches the series.

The guide provides scaffolding for individual learning needs. The activities in the guide help students access prior knowledge and make connections to new learning, while also providing students with additional experience using key words.

The activities featured in this Teacher's Guide are flexible and varied. Many can be adapted to suit whole-class, small-group, or independent learning situations with different instruction schedules. A variety of written and oral word games provides students more practice with familiar and key vocabulary words from the lessons. These games include limericks and other poems; rhyming riddles; dictionary games; anagrams; coded messages; jokes and puns; and crossword puzzles.

Lesson Format

Every lesson has the following format:

Literary and Historical References

INTRODUCE Lesson

PREVIEW Familiar Words

PRESENT Key Words

GUIDE Practice

Key Word Activity Master

ASSIGN Exercises

REVIEW Lessons (after every two lessons)

SELECT Review Exercises (after every two lessons)

Literary and Historical References

Many of the illustrative sentences refer to literary works or historical events. For your convenience, a list of the references is included at the start of each lesson. You may wish to discuss them with your students when the reference appears in a sentence.

INTRODUCE Lesson

Introduce or review the theme of each lesson pair by displaying, reading, and translating the opening quotation for each lesson and connecting the quote to the lesson content.

PREVIEW Familiar Words

Help students make connections with familiar words that have the same roots as the new words they will be learning about in the lesson. The goal of the preview section is to access students' prior knowledge in order to build a context for learning new, related words.

PRESENT Key Words

Display the roots from the lesson and give their meanings. Read the list of new key words chorally from the student book. Key words are presented through discussion of pronunciation, definition and connection to the root, example sentences, parts of speech, and word forms. Special *Nota Bene* sections are discussed in detail.

GUIDE Practice

Participate with students in a short, interactive activity that reinforces the meanings of the key words.

Key Word Activity Master

Further reinforce the meanings of the key words. It can be completed as an independent, small-group, or whole-class activity. There is one reproducible master for each lesson; they are all located at the end of the Teacher's Guide.

ASSIGN Exercises

Assign student book exercises. Suggestions for how to complete these exercises can be found on page vii.

REVIEW Lessons

Review words from the previous two lessons in this interactive activity.

SELECT Review Exercises

Assign student book review exercises. Suggestions for how to complete these exercises can be found on page vii.

Additional Vocabulary Games and Activities

Here are some suggestions for reinforcement and review.

Scavenger Hunt

Ask members of competing teams where they would go to find a specific person or object indicated by a key word from the lesson. For example, "Where in the school would you go to find a *copious* supply of pencils?" Possible answer: the supply closet.

Pantomime/Charades

Have students act out a key word. The rest of the students try to guess the correct word.

Quick on the Draw/Pictorial Charades

Divide students into two teams. One student from each team sketches a picture of a target word while his or her teammates try to guess what word is being drawn. The first team to guess correctly gets a point.

Creating Words

Have students create new words using one or more of the roots from the lesson. Students can also provide a definition, an illustrative sentence, and/or an illustration of the word. For example, a student who studied the roots *micro* (meaning "small") and *bovis* (meaning "cow") might create the word *microbovis*, define it as "a really tiny breed of cattle," and draw a picture of a tiny cow. Have the students display their created words for the rest of the class.

Root Bingo

To review several lessons, create a number of different bingo boards (3x3 or 5x5 grid), filling in the boxes with Greek and Latin roots from the various lessons. Give each student a board and provide bingo chips or other markers. Write the key words and their definitions on cards, then put them in a container. Pull out a card, and read the word and the definition. Students place a bingo chip on the root from which that word derives.

Flashcards

Have students write the key word on the front of a note card and the definition on the back. Students can review these words independently or with a partner.

Sorts

Using flashcards, students sort words by common roots and then state the definition of each word.

Additional Word-Learning Strategies and Activities

When students will benefit from a more in-depth exploration of a vocabulary word, the following word-learning strategies and activities may be helpful. These strategies can be especially useful for content-area terminology— vocabulary words with connections to social studies, science, or math.

Root Webs

A root web can help students identify origins and meanings that are common to a group of words. Display the root in the middle of the web and discuss its meaning. Complete the rest of the web with words that include that root. This can include different forms of the same word. Discuss definitions and relationship of the word to the root. Also, clarify confusing words that may appear to include the root but have other origins; for example, the word "tricky" has the letters *t, r,* and *i* at the beginning but does not relate to the number three.

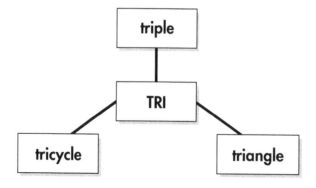

Comparing and Contrasting Words or Concepts with Venn Diagrams

A Venn diagram is especially useful in helping students understand the relationship among content area concepts through comparison and contrast. For example, the following Venn diagram can help show the differences and similarities between a *monarch* and a *magnate*. The overlap of the circles shows what qualities are shared.

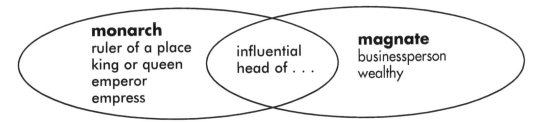

Concept of Definition Maps

Concept of Definition maps are visual displays that show the common components of a dictionary definition. Students can use context, prior knowledge, and dictionaries to fill in the map as they answer the following questions:

- *What is it?*
- *What is it like?*
- *What are some specific examples of the word?*
- *What are some specific nonexamples of the word?*

Independently or in groups, students fill in the map then use the information on the map to write a definition of the key word. The following map clarifies the meaning of the word *monarch*.

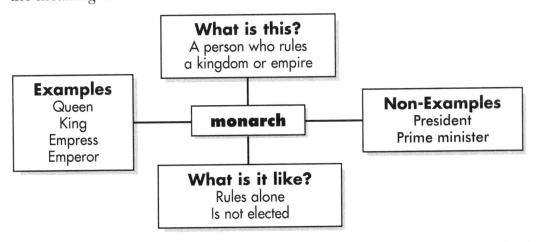

Students then use the map to write a definition for the word. For example, *A monarch is a ruler of a kingdom or empire. A monarch rules alone and is not elected by people. Some kinds of monarchs are queens, kings, and emperors.*

Word Building and Parts of Speech

Ask students to add an array of affixes to word roots to create long words. For example, ask students to create as many words as they can by combining the root *vis* with the affixes *-ible, in-,* and *-ity.* Then have students use the dictionary to determine each word's part of speech. For more of a challenge, have students mix and match word parts. For example, ask students what real words they can make with the morphemes *vise, pro-, -gress, -ion, re-.* Then have students use the dictionary to determine each word's part of speech.

Suggestions For Completing Student Book Exercises

The following directions can provide additional help to students.

General Suggestions

For each exercise, read the directions and underline, circle, or highlight important words (*synonym, antonym, used incorrectly, most appropriate*) that indicate how to complete the exercise.

Exercise A: Synonyms and Antonyms

Synonyms: When the directions say to circle the letter of the word or phrase MOST NEARLY THE SAME as the word in boldfaced type, substitute each suggested answer for the boldfaced word to see if that answer makes sense in that phrase. Pay attention to any context clues in the phrase that may help to choose the correct word. Cross out any answers that do not make sense. Ask whether the chosen word has the same or nearly the same meaning as the boldfaced word.

Antonyms: When the directions say to circle the letter of the word or phrase MOST NEARLY THE OPPOSITE to the word in boldfaced type, take the boldfaced word out of the sentence. Ask whether the chosen word has the opposite or nearly the opposite meaning to the boldfaced word. Cross out any answers that do not make sense.

Exercise B: Incorrect Usage

Read each sentence, paying particular attention to context clues. Consult the definition of the word as necessary, paying particular attention to multiple meanings. Find the one sentence in which the boldfaced key word is not used properly. If completing this in class, discuss answers with partners or in small groups.

Exercise C: Fill-in-the-Blank

Read the entire sentence and highlight any context clues. Look at the key words, and determine which ones might relate to the context clues. Rule out any obvious incorrect answers. Then substitute possible answers for the blank and read the sentence to decide which word fits best.

Review Exercises

Analogies

Analogies in *Vocabulary from Classical Roots* usually focus on discovering the relationship between two given roots or words. Sometimes the roots or words provided are synonyms or antonyms. Sometimes a key word and a root are provided. The first step in solving analogies is to know what each root or word means. Look back at the definitions in the beginning of the lesson. If the relationship is not immediately clear, it helps to create a sentence that describes the relationship between the given word pair. Use that same sentence to solve the other half of the analogy. Modify the relationship sentence as needed in order to create a sentence that will work in both pairs of words.

Writing or Discussion Activities

Exercises can be completed individually, in pairs, or small groups. If done in pairs, each group of students should have its own question and should present its answers in a whole-group discussion.

Scheduling Instruction in Your Classroom

The organization of the lessons can accommodate a variety of instructional schedules. Some of the shorter activities can be combined to create longer lessons. Other activities can be assigned as homework according to class schedule and individual needs. This table of approximate completion times will help you manage your vocabulary instruction schedule.

	Description	Approximate completion time	Need student book?
1.	INTRODUCE Lesson X	5 minutes	No
2.	PREVIEW Familiar Words	10-15 minutes	No
3.	PRESENT Key Words	20 minutes	Yes
4.	GUIDE Practice	15 minutes	Optional
5.	Key Word Activity Master*	15 minutes	Optional
6.	ASSIGN Exercises*	30 minutes	Yes
7.	REVIEW Lessons X and X	15 minutes	Optional
8.	SELECT Review Exercises	15 minutes	Yes

* Can be assigned as homework

Keep in mind that if you will be using the *Vocabulary from Classical Roots* tests, they need to be incorporated into your instructional schedule.

LESSON 1

Literary and Historical References

3. creditable During the Civil War Dorothea Dix (1802–1887) organized "plain-looking and respectable" women to tend the sick and wounded. Their success overcame then-current prejudices against women serving in military hospitals.

4. credulous The protagonist of *The Adventures of Tom Sawyer* by Samuel Clemens (1835–1910) is notorious for his skills as a juvenile "con artist."

5. creed These lines are from "The Pilgrim Forefathers" by American author Helen Hunt Jackson (1830–1885), who is best known for her novel *Ramona*.

6. deify To emphasize their divine ancestry, pharaohs are often depicted in painting and statuary either as Horus or with Horus, the ancient Egyptian sun god represented with the head of a hawk.

7. deity To insure fertility, first-born children and animals were sacrificed to Astarte (referred to in the Bible as Ashtoreth, a Philistine goddess), who was represented by cow's horns. Her cult spread through the eastern Mediterranean, where it merged with that of Aphrodite in Greek areas.

9. divinity Shakespeare's *King Lear* contrasts the loving Cordelia, who is punished for her refusal to make hyperbolic protestations of love for her father, with her lying sisters, who lavishly proclaim their love and then abuse the powerless old king.

11. theocracy The present Dalai Lama, Tenzin Gyatso (b. 1935), whom his followers regard as the fourteenth incarnation of Avalokitesvara, bodhisattva of compassion, lives in exile in the Indian city of Dharmsala. Winner of the 1989 Nobel Peace Prize, the Dalai Lama speaks and writes widely on nonviolence and spirituality.

13. atheist Known in school as the "Eton Atheist," poet Percy Bysshe Shelley (1792–1822) was expelled from Oxford in 1811 for circulating a pamphlet, "The Necessity of Atheism," written by a close friend.

14. pantheism American poet Walt Whitman (1819–1892) is best known for his poetry collected in *Leaves of Grass* (1855), of which "Song of Myself" is the opening poem.

Exercise 1B, 1a Augurs, official Roman diviners, considered the numbers, call, pattern and direction of flight, and related behavior of birds to be significant signs for predicting the outcome of an undertaking.

Exercise 1B, 1b Quetzalcoatl, the Toltec and Aztec god of winds and the breath of life, is associated with fertility and regarded as a divine king and cultural hero who taught human beings the calendar and crafts.

Exercise 1B, 1d Joseph, the biblical hero of Genesis 37-50, won the Pharaoh's favor by interpreting the ruler's dream as a prediction of famine and then managing the ensuing crisis.

Exercise 1B, 2b In Shakespeare's *As You Like It*, Rosalind's frank and sensible attitude toward love makes Orlando's lovesickness seem silly.

Exercise 1B, 2c In her curiosity to know the identity of her mysterious husband, Cupid, who visits her only under cover of darkness, Psyche accidentally harms him and thus angers his mother, Aphrodite. To appease the goddess and prove her love for Cupid, she endures many tests that ultimately win her deification.

Exercise 1B, 3a The word *manitou* is derived from the Algonquian language and refers to a mysterious cosmic force believed to exist everywhere in nature.

Exercise 1B, 3b During most of the Roman Empire's existence, conquered peoples were free to practice their own religions as long as they also acknowledged and made sacrifices to the Roman gods, including deified emperors.

Exercise 1B, 3d The gods of the classical Greek period were largely associated with natural forces; particular local sites, such as groves, streams, or hilltops, were commonly ascribed to gods favored in that vicinity.

Exercise 1B, 5b A god of agriculture and fertility, Dagon was worshipped by the Phoenicians and is probably identical with Dagan, god of the Babylonians and Assyrians.

Exercise 1B, 5c Islam is adamantly monotheistic, recognizing Allah as sole supreme being and Muhammad as only a mortal prophet.

Exercise 1B, 5d One of the greatest achievements of the classical period of Mayan culture, A.D. 300–900, Mayan astronomy seems to have arisen from a need to determine the precise timing of religious rituals based on the movement of heavenly bodies.

Exercise 1C, 1	This phrase is attributed to Phineas Taylor Barnum (1810–1891), "the Prince of Humbugs" and entrepreneur of "the greatest show on earth." He was one of the first impresarios to capitalize on mass publicity and the gullibility of the public.
Exercise 1C, 5	A fundamental precept of Hinduism and Buddhism, *karma* is the life experience allotted to an individual as a consequence of that person's previous existences. The karmic system assumes a reincarnation of the soul and has as its ultimate goal *nirvana,* the release of the soul from repeated rebirth.
Exercise 1C, 7	The Lascaux caves, located near Montignac in the Dordogne area of France, contain famous prehistoric paintings of animals such as horses, bison, stags, and cows that date from 15,000 B.C.
Exercise 1C, 11	Said to have "a fierce and courageous temper," Anne Bonny eloped from her family's South Carolina plantation with the notorious pirate "Calico Jack" Rackham and shared his exploits. Mary Read joined their crew when the merchant ship where she served, disguised as a man, was captured by Rackham and Bonny. When the pirates were captured in 1820, both women falsely pleaded pregnancy but were eventually hanged.

INTRODUCE Lesson 1

(Book D, page 3)

Tell students that the theme of Lessons 1 and 2 is "Believing."

Display, read, and translate this Latin phrase (from page 3 of Lesson 1): *Crede quod habes, et habes.* "Believe that you have it, and you have it."

- Ask students for their ideas about what the phrase means. What do they think someone might have by believing he or she has it? (Samples: confidence, beauty)
- Ask which Latin word in the phrase means "believe." (*Crede*)
- Tell students that English words with the root *cred* are among the words to learn in Lesson 1.

PREVIEW Familiar Words

(Book D, pages 4–5)

credit, discredit, incredible, divine, monotheism

ACTIVITY 1

The Latin *credere* ("to believe") and related forms are sources of English words with the root *cred*. Help students compare and contrast words with the root.

Display the familiar words *credit, discredit,* and *incredible.*

Remind students that the root *cred* means "believe."

Discuss definitions of the three words, including how prefixes change meaning (Samples: *credit* means "trust or *belief* in"; to *discredit* is to show why someone shouldn't be *believed; incredible* means un*believable.*)

ACTIVITY 2

The Latin *divinare* ("to foretell") and related forms are sources of English words with the root *divin*. Help students understand that other meanings have grown from the root.

Display the familiar word *divine.*

Read aloud the phrases below, and discuss what *divine* means in each one:

- use a *divining* rod (a forked rod believed to indicate the presence of water or minerals)
- the *divine* right of kings (the right to rule granted by a supernatural power)
- a dessert that is simply *divine* (wonderful, heavenly)

Ask: What do you think is the meaning of the root *divin* from these sentences? ("foretelling" for the first one; "godlike" for the last two)

Tell students that the adjective *divine* can describe a being, state, or thing that has godlike qualities. The original Latin root actually means "to foretell"; the meaning connection is that ancient Romans looked to their gods to foretell future events.

ACTIVITY 3

The Greek *theos* ("god") is the source of English words with the root *the(o)*. Help students think about word parts and root meaning.

Display the familiar word *monotheism.*

Say this sentence, and have students use context to tell what monotheism is: A religion developed that was based on *monotheism,* rather than on the worship of many gods. (belief in one God)

Have students identify the prefix that means "one" (*mono-*), the suffix that means "belief or practice" (*-ism*), and the root that means "god" (*the*).

ACTIVITY 4: Nouns and Verbs

Tell students that the adjective meaning of *divine* is more familiar than the verb meaning, which they will learn in Lesson 1. Focus on parts of speech by having partners look up the word *credit* in a dictionary and use the definitions to write two sentences with *credit* as a noun and two as a verb. Then take turns reading aloud their sentences and have classmates identify the part of speech.

ACTIVITY 5: Review Familiar Words

Review by having students give a meaning for the Lesson 1 roots *cred* ("believe"), *divin* ("foretell"), and *theo(s)* ("god"). Lesson 1 also includes the Latin *deus* ("god"), which is the source of English words with the root *dei*.

PRESENT Key Words

(Book D, pages 3–6)

Direct students to read the four root families boldfaced on pages 4–5 of their Level D books. Then have them turn to page 3 to read the boxed key words chorally: *accredit, apotheosis, atheist, credence, creditable, credulous, creed, deify, deity, divine, divinity, pantheism, pantheon, theocracy, theology.*

Present each key word by discussing the following:

- pronunciation
- definitions/connections to the root
- sentences
- parts of speech
- word forms

Point out the antonyms *credulous* and *incredulous*, and have students tell what the prefix *in-* means in this case ("not, opposite of"). Ask them to imagine that they have just been told some surprising news; have them demonstrate a *credulous* reaction and an *incredulous* reaction.

GUIDE Practice

Categories

Have students name the key word or words that belong in each list, and tell what the words have in common:

- praiseworthy, reputable, deserving, (creditable; all are favorable descriptions of accomplishments or people)
- goddess, immortal one, supreme being, (divinity, deity; all name gods or supernatural beings)
- certify, authorize, license, (accredit; all mean "to show official recognition")
- faith, principle, viewpoint, (creed; all are types of beliefs)

- science, literature, language, (theology; all name fields of study)
- recommendation, credential, trustworthiness, (credence; all relate to trusting or believing someone)
- exalt, worship, glorify, (deify; all are ways to treat someone like a god)
- exaltation, hero worship, glorification, (apotheosis; all are names for making someone godlike)
- devout person, believer, nonbeliever, (atheist; all name people who have a chosen view of religion)
- creed, theology, monotheism, (pantheism; all are systems of belief)
- democracy, dictatorship, monarchy, (theocracy; all are systems of government)
- deities, divinities, guardian angels, (pantheon; all are names for the gods or spirits of a religion)
- gullible, naive, trusting, (credulous; all describe people who can be easily fooled)
- guess, predict, tell fortunes (divine; all are ways to try to predict the future)

Lesson 1 Key Word Activity Master (see page 115)

Answers:

1. pantheism
2. accreditation
3. credence
4. divine
5. deify
6. theologians
7. creed
8. atheist
9. credulous
10. deities
11. divinity
12. pantheon
13. creditably
14. apotheosis
15. theocratically

ASSIGN Exercises

(Book D, pages 7–10)

LESSON 2

Literary and Historical References

1. consecrate — Lincoln delivered this famous speech on November 19, 1863, at the dedication of the national cemetery on the battlefield at Gettysburg, where the decisive battle of the Civil War had been fought just four months earlier.

2. execrate — The Incas of South America mined gold, the symbol of their sun god, primarily for decorative and ritual purposes, not as a medium of exchange. Their conquerors, however, appreciated the gold artifacts only for their monetary value.

3. sacrament — These lines occur in the poem "Peter Quince at the Clavier" by Wallace Stevens (1879–1955).

4. sacrilege — During his short term of office as Archbishop of Canterbury, William Temple (1881–1944) became increasingly concerned with social, economic, and international issues.

5. sacrosanct — This novel by Rudolfo Anaya (b. 1937) concerns a young Chicano's coming of age in the rural Southwest during the 1940s.

8. sanctity — Canadian poet John Gillespie Magee, Jr., (1922–1941) died during World War II.

11. hieroglyphic — Recent research has recognized Mayan hieroglyphics, originally thought to be unintelligible pictographs, as a system that combines phonetic and ideogrammatic symbols.

13. piety — These lines appear in the 1802 poem "My Heart Leaps Up" by William Wordsworth (1770–1850).

Exercise 2B, 1a — Economic sanctions imposed by the United Nations, the United States, the European Economic Community, and other governmental organizations had only a limited effect in ending apartheid, the laws of which were revoked during the early 1990s.

Exercise 2B, 1b — Because Charles V, the Holy Roman Emperor and nephew of English Queen Catherine of Aragon, dominated Italy at the time, Pope Clement VII refused the request of Henry VIII to divorce his barren wife and marry Anne Boleyn (1507–1536), by whom he hoped to have an heir.

Exercise 2B, 2a — Priestesses of the temple of Vesta in Rome, the vestal virgins were selected for this office as young girls and served for thirty years during which time they were expected to maintain absolute chastity.

Exercise 2B, 2b   Fearing that the French Revolution (1789–1815) might inspire similar violence against the lives and property of their own monarch and nobility, British leaders opposed the Revolution.

Exercise 2B, 2c   In *The Hunchback of Notre Dame* by Victor Hugo (1802–1885), Quasimodo, the deformed bell ringer of the cathedral, helps the gypsy girl Esmerelda to escape a mob who accuse her of witchcraft, but she is later tricked into leaving sanctuary, attacked, and hanged.

Exercise 2B, 3a   In *The Scarlet Letter*, which Nathaniel Hawthorne (1804–1864) set in Puritan New England, Hester Prynne is forced to wear the *A* to mark her as an adulterer, but her lover, the guilt-ridden Reverend Arthur Dimmesdale, hides his sin until his dying confession.

Exercise 2B, 3b   The conciliatory and nonviolent policies of Mahatma Gandhi (1869– 1948) helped win independence for India, but his dream of a single state uniting Hindus and Muslims failed when the Muslim state of Pakistan was partitioned from India.

Exercise 2B, 4c   In Shakespeare's *Macbeth*, Macbeth is goaded by his own ambitions and his wife to murder King Duncan and usurp the throne, an act in direct defiance of the principle of the divine right of kings to rule.

Exercise 2B, 4d   Because of their belief in karma (see entry for Exercise 1C, 5), Hindus believe that all animals possess a soul, which may have been human in a previous incarnation.

Exercise 2B, 5d   The religious life of the Hopis of Arizona centers on the kachina cult and ceremonies associated with the seasons of the year. Supernatural beings believed to bring rain and general well-being to the Hopis, kachinas often are represented by sacred dolls.

Exercise 2B, 6b   Amaterasu Omikami, the Japanese sun goddess and principal deity, is said to have sprung from the left eye of Izanagi, the male of the Heavenly Pair who together created Japan and from whom all Japanese are said to descend.

Exercise 2B, 6d   The protagonist of *The Mayor of Casterbridge* by Thomas Hardy (1840–1928), Michael Henchard feels he can never expiate the guilt he incurs for selling his wife and child in a drunken rage.

Exercise 2C, 1   Italian-born Marisa Bellisario joined Olivetti when she graduated from the Turin University in 1960; she rose rapidly through the ranks from systems analyst to director of the Olivetti Company's branch in the United States.

Exercise 2C, 2	The Chinese sage Confucius (551–479 B.C.), also known as Kung Chui or Kung Fu-tse, used the orderly, tradition-respecting hierarchical family as an emblem of the well-governed state.
Exercise 2C, 6	The satirical novels of Evelyn Waugh (1903–1966) portray the cynicism and superficiality of English society between the world wars; later works like *Brideshead Revisited* capture the disillusionment of the postwar era.
Exercise 2C, 7	*The Oresteia* by Aeschylus (525–456 B.C.) is the only surviving trilogy of Greek tragedies. In *Agamemnon*, the first play, Agamemnon is murdered by Clytemnestra, his unfaithful wife; in the second, *The Libation Bearers*, his son Orestes avenges his death by murdering Clytemnestra. In the final play, *The Eumenides*, Athena helps Orestes to purge himself of the pollution resulting from paricide.
Exercise 2C, 11	A succession of young girls is chosen to embody the Living Goddess, a cult native to the Kathmandu Valley of Nepal; each reigning goddess lives in her temple attended with great wealth and circumstance, and at maturity retires with a large dowry but poor prospects, for former goddesses are considered bad marriage partners.

INTRODUCE Lesson 2

(Book D, page 10)

Remind students that the theme of Lessons 1 and 2 is "Believing."

Display, read, and translate this Latin phrase (from page 10 of Lesson 2): *Sanctus, sanctus, sanctus.* "Holy, holy, holy."

- Tell students that the quotation is from the book Revelation of the New Testament of the Bible, and that Latin is closely associated with Roman Catholicism. Ask students for examples of other languages associated with different religions. (Samples: Hebrew/Yiddish with Judaism; Arabic with Islam; Japanese with Shintoism)
- Explain that English words with the root sanct—meaning "holy—are among the words to learn in Lesson 2.

PREVIEW Familiar Words

(Book D, page 10)

sacred, sacrifice, sacrificial

ACTIVITY 1

The Latin root *sacer* ("sacred") is the source of English words with the root *sacr*. Help students make meaning connections.

Display the familiar words *sacred, sacrifice, sacrificial.*

Have students offer sentences that include the word *holy* along with each listed word. (Samples: A *sacred* vow is *holy.*/A *holy sacrifice* is an offering to a deity, and it can also be called a *sacrificial* offering.)

Review by having students tell how knowing the meaning of the root will help them make educated guesses about new words that include *sacr.* (Sample: The words will relate to a higher purpose or selfless act.)

ACTIVITY 2: Multiple Meanings

Have students share their knowledge of the word *sacrifice* in each of these contexts. Use a dictionary if necessary:

a *sacrifice* fly in baseball (Sample: an out purposely made by a player to advance his or her teammate)

to *sacrifice* profits in business (Sample: to sell at a loss of profit)

to *sacrifice* one's pride (Sample: to put aside pride for a higher goal)

parents' *sacrifices* for their children (Sample: things a parent gives up for the good of the children)

ACTIVITY 3: Review Familiar Words

Review by having students give the meaning of the root *sacer* ("sacred"). Lesson 2 also includes the roots *sanctus* (Latin for "holy"), source of English words with the root *sanct*; the Greek *hieros* ("holy"), source of English words with the root *hier*; and the Latin *piare* ("to purify [with sacred rites]"), source of English words with the root *pi(e)* (piety, impious)

PRESENT Key Words

(Book D, pages 10–14)

Direct students to read the four roots and root families boldfaced on pages 10–13 of their Level D books. Then have them turn to page 10 to read the boxed key words chorally: *consecrate, execrate, expiate, hierarchy, hieroglyphic, impious, piety, pittance, sacrament, sacrilege, sacrosanct, sanctimonious, sanction, sanctity, sanctuary.*

- Present each key word by discussing the following:
- pronunciation
- definitions/connections to the root
- sentences
- parts of speech
- word forms

Use the *Nota Bene* for *sanction* to make the point that English has a few words that can have opposite meanings. The word *sanction* entered English from a Latin word for "sacred law." Because such a law could both punish and permit, a sanction can refer to both punishment and permission.

Use the *Nota Bene* for *sanctuary* to point out how a word may start with a specific meaning—an accused person's privilege of sanctuary in a church—and develop broader meanings over time. Today, speakers may talk about seeking *sanctuary* in a quiet garden or strolling through a bird *sanctuary*.

Point out the antonyms *piety/impiety* and *pious/impious*, and have students tell what the prefix *im-* means in these words ("not, opposite of"). Explain that the prefix *in-* is assimilated, or changes its spelling, to *im-* before the consonants *b, m,* and *p.*

GUIDE Practice

True or False

Have students hold thumbs up for each true statement and thumbs down for each false statement. Use root meanings or definitions to discuss their reasoning, then restate each false statement as a true one:

- A house of worship is one place to show *piety*. (True; a house of worship is a place to demonstrate *respect* and *devotion*, to *appease* the gods.)
- A *sanctimonious* attitude deserves respect. (False; someone who is sanctimonious only *pretends* to be *holy*.)
- An example of *impious* behavior is chatting loudly during a lecture. (True; it is *disrespectful* to chat while others are talking, and would thus not [indicated by the prefix im-] *appease* the speaker.)
- A reviewer who *execrates* a book is recommending it. (False; the reviewer is *denouncing* the book.)
- We can see *hieroglyphic* forms in ancient Egyptian tombs. (True; ancient tombs display early communication as *sacred carvings*.)
- It is difficult to live well on a *pittance*. (True; a pittance is a *meager portion*.)
- In a *hierarchical* organization, everyone has an equal say. (False; a hierarchy *ranks* members.)
- Actions that are *expiated* are made to speed up. (False; expiation implies *atonement*, not rapidity.)
- Destroying tombstones is a *sacrilege*. (True; destroying tombstones is *disrespectful* to something regarded as *sacred*.)
- Land is open to development only after it is *consecrated*. (False; consecrated land is seen as *sacred*, and is protected from development.)
- A book could be *sacrosanct*. (True; some books are considered *holy*. The Bible is *sacrosanct* to many. Collectors hold the first Superman comic book to be *sacrosanct*.)
- People who display *sanctity* are often unkind to their neighbors. (False; sanctity means *holiness* and implies the person will be kind to his or her neighbor.)

- People who need *sanctuary* may be looking for safety. (True; a sanctuary is a place of *refuge.*)
- Parents generally *sanction* activities that help their children learn. (True; most parents *support* educational activities.)
- Baptism is an example of a Christian *sacrament.* (True; Baptism is considered to have a *sacred* significance.)

Lesson 2 Key Word Activity Master (see page 116)

Answers:

1. attempts to expiate
2. consecration
3. piety
4. a pittance
5. a sanctuary
6. a sanctioned performance
7. a sanctimonious manner
8. the top of the hierarchy
9. impious behavior
10. his sacrosanct spot
11. a hieroglyphic system
12. a place of sanctity
13. sacramental robes
14. an execrable sacrilege

ASSIGN Exercises

Book D, pages 14–17

REVIEW Lessons 1 and 2

Ask a student to read aloud each of the thirty key words while listeners take turns explaining its meaning connection to its root. For example: *When you expiate a sin, you perform an act to "purify" yourself./Something that is sacrosanct is "sacred" and "holy."* For words in which the meaning connection is not apparent (*pittance*, for example), have a student use a dictionary to read aloud the derivation.

SELECT Review Exercises

Book D, pages 17–19

LESSON 3

Literary and Historical References

1. dogma
In *Hard Times* by Charles Dickens (1812–1870), Mr. Gradgrind runs an experimental school where only facts are taught. Through him Dickens expresses his criticism of nineteenth-century industrialization and utilitarianism.

2. dogmatic
Influenced by the theory of Georg Wilhelm Friedrich Hegel (1770–1831) that human events result from the dialectic of opposing forces, Karl Marx (1818–1883) regarded class conflict between the bourgeoisie, who control means of production, and the workers, or proletariat, as an inevitable fact of social evolution.

In *Brave New World* by Aldous Huxley (1894–1963), new generations are cloned in test tubes and programmed from their "decantation" to fit into assigned niches in a hierarchical society that depends on avid consumerism.

3. heterodox
Many of the ideas and practices of Sigmund Freud (1856–1939), such as his theoretical formulation of the unconscious and especially his theories of libido and infant sexuality, initially met with disdain and outrage by the medical profession at the turn of the century.

5. physiognomy
In his description of the Wife of Bath, who has already had "five husbands at church door" but is looking for another, Geoffrey Chaucer (1343–1400) reflects a belief popular when he wrote *The Canterbury Tales* and still current today—that being gap-toothed is a sign of sensuality.

8. hypocrisy
Lily Bart, protagonist of *The House of Mirth* by Edith Wharton (1862– 1937), epitomizes the debutante who cannot survive without finding a wealthy husband; although rejected by aristocratic New York society and unable to support herself, Lily dies with her integrity intact.

11. frenetic
In his classic film *Modern Times* (1936), Charlie Chaplin (1889–1977) depicts with humor the twentieth-century plight of the "little guy" opposing the "big machine."

Although the protagonist of *Anna Karenina* by Leo Tolstoy (1828–1910) escapes a sterile marriage to live with her lover, Count Vronsky, she finds no peace. She is tormented by jealousy, grief over the loss of her son, and self-destructiveness that finally ends in suicide.

12. schizophrenia Dick Diver, the protagonist of *Tender is the Night* (1934) by F. Scott Fitzgerald (1896–1940), embodies the psychological and spiritual malaise of society between the world wars.

The novels and stories of Caribbean writer Jamaica Kincaid (b. 1949) often depict the tensions between the culture of her native island and that of Western industrial society.

13. arraign Susette La Flesche, using her Native American name of Inshtateamba, or "Bright Eyes," began speaking on behalf of the Ponca people who were forced off their lands and whose leaders were jailed in 1877. As a direct result of her efforts, Senator Henry L. Dawes sponsored legislation in 1887 protecting Native American rights.

15. rationalize Twice rejected by Harvard but later trained by a British practitioner, Harriot K. Hunt (1805–1875) practiced medicine in Boston without a license from 1834 until her death. She was awarded an honorary M.D. by the Female Medical College of Pennsylvania.

Exercise 3B, 2b The poetry of Robert Frost (1874–1963) is noted for its focus on the individual and its observations of New England rural life.

Exercise 3B, 2c Although generally presented as an officious busybody, Polonius, King Claudius's lord chamberlain in Shakespeare's *Hamlet,* is allowed one fleeting moment of wisdom and high poetry in his speech of advice to his departing son.

Exercise 3B, 3a Although *Northanger Abbey* appeared posthumously in 1819, it is probably the earliest work by Jane Austen (1775–1817).

Exercise 3B, 3c In *The Canterbury Tales,* the Pardoner confides, "My theme is always the same and ever was: *Radix malorum est Cupiditas"* (The love of money is the root of all evil).

Exercise 3B, 4d Pythia, the priestess of Apollo at Delphi, is known to have made her prophetic utterances seated on a tripod and holding a spray of laurel, but no contemporary descriptions reveal the exact process.

Exercise 3B, 5b The "uncertainty principle" of German physicist Werner Heisenberg (1901–1976) states that there are fundamental limits on knowledge of nature at the atomic level, including the fact that observation alters phenomena.

Exercise 3B, 5c Although originally a Puritan, Anne Hutchinson (1591–1643) challenged the political and religious system of the Massachusetts colony by arguing the authority of personal revelation over civil powers; ultimately banished from the colony, she helped to establish the first settlement in Rhode Island.

Exercise 3B, 7a	His biting lampoons of the French regency and his relentless attacks on the church so offended those in power that Voltaire (François-Marie Arouet, 1694–1778) was imprisoned in the Bastille and later forced to live most of his life in exile.
Exercise 3B, 7c	Arrested in 1660 for preaching without a license, which was granted only to members of the "established church," Baptist John Bunyan (1628–1688) spent the next twelve years in Bedford jail, where he wrote nine books.
Exercise 3B, 8d	The nineteenth-century "scientist" Johann Casper Spurzheim popularized phrenology (not frenetics) as a method of gaining insights into personality by examining the shape of the skull, but by the end of the century increased knowledge of the brain and nervous system had discredited his theories.
Exercise 3B, 9b	Lord Peter Wimsey, the amateur detective created by Dorothy L. Sayers (1893–1957), first meets his future wife Harriet Vane when she is tried for murder in the novel *Strong Poison*.
Exercise 3B, 9c	Dorothea Dix (1802–1887) worked to improve conditions in mental institutions and prisons (see entry for Lesson 1, 3).
Exercise 3C, 4	Because Ham has seen his father Noah drunk and naked, Noah condemns Ham's son to servitude (Genesis 9:20-27).
Exercise 3C, 5	English composer Ralph Vaughan Williams (1872–1958) drew upon English folk traditions and Renaissance music to create his uniquely English style.
Exercise 3C, 6	Having been introduced to tennis in Bermuda in 1874, Mary Ewing Outerbridge brought equipment home with her to Staten Island, New York, where she and her brothers popularized the game in East Coast high society.
Exercise 3C, 8	The Shahada is one of the "five pillars of Islam"; reciting it before witnesses is the only requirement for becoming a Muslim.

INTRODUCE Lesson 3

(Book D, page 20)

Tell students that the theme of Lessons 3 and 4 is "Thinking and Knowing."

Display, read, and translate this Latin quotation (from page 20 of Lesson 3): *Cogito, ergo sum.* "I think; therefore I am."

- Explain that this famous statement in Latin was used by the French philosopher René Descartes (1596–1650) to express his idea that the ability to think, question, and reason gives meaning to people's lives. Ask students if they have heard this phrase before, if so, where, and what they think of it.
- Tell students that Lesson 3 presents English words with Latin and Greek roots having to do with thinking, reasoning, forming opinions, and using the mind.

PREVIEW Familiar Words

(Book D, pages 21–24)

crisis, critic, amnesia, frantic, frenzy, rational, irrational

ACTIVITY 1

The Greek *krinein* ("to separate," "to decide," "to judge") is the source of English words with the root *cris/crit*. Help students compare and contrast words with the root.

Display the familiar words *crisis* and *critic*.

Read aloud the sentences below with the emphasis shown. Direct students to complete the sentences:

- In a crisis, good judgment is important because… (Sample: It is easy to panic when flustered, but it's very important to stay calm and think clearly in order to deal with the problem.)
- A critic is like a judge because… (Sample: The opinion of a critic can help determine the future of whatever is being reviewed.)

Tell students that the roots *cris* and *crit* come from a Greek word that means "to judge."

ACTIVITY 2

The Greek *mnemonikos* ("mindful") is the source of English words with the root *mne*. Help students make meaning connections.

Display the familiar word *amnesia*.

Ask several students to describe the state of *amnesia*. Every time the word *memory* or *remember* is mentioned, write *mne* on the chalkboard.

Ask: When and why am I writing *mne*? (Sample: It was listed each time someone used a word having to do with memory.)

Point out that the Greek root *mne* appears in words having to do with memory or remembering, but that the meaning of the Greek root *mnemonikos* is actually "mindful."

ACTIVITY 3

The Greek *phren* ("mind") is the source of English words with the root *fren/fran/phren*. Help students think about the root meaning.

Display the familiar words *frantic* and *frenzy*.

- Ask students to use both words in a sentence that shows their understanding of word meaning. (Sample: I felt *frantic* because I was so late, so I went into a *frenzy* of activity.)
- Ask: What do you think the Greek root meaning "mind" has to do with the meanings of *frantic* and *frenzy*? (Sample: When you are frantic or in a frenzy, your mind is racing.)

ACTIVITY 4

The Latin *ratio* ("reason") and related forms are sources of English words with the root *ratio*. Help students think about the root meaning.

Display the familiar words *rational* and *irrational*.

Underline *ratio* in each, explaining that the spelling of the root in English is the same as the Latin word for "reason."

Tell students that *ratio*, *rational* numbers, and *irrational* numbers are all terms used in mathematics. Ask students to make a meaning connection between the root "reason" and the study of math. (Samples: You need to use logic and *reasoning* when approaching a math problem./Math studies the *reasons* numbers interact the way they do.)

ACTIVITY 5: Fill-in-the-Blank

Have students fill in the blanks with their own ideas of thinking and knowing. Have them sign their statements, then read some aloud for students to guess the authors' identities:

_____; ergo _____./I _____; therefore I _____.

Example: I think; therefore I write poetry.

Example: I exercise, therefore I am strong.

ACTIVITY 6: Review Familiar Words

Review by having students give a meaning for the Lesson 3 roots *cris/crit* ("to judge"); *mne* ("mindful"); *fran/fren* ("mind"); and *ratio* ("reason"). Lesson 3 also includes the Greek *dokein* ("to appear," "to seem," "to think") and *doxa* ("opinion," "judgment"), which are sources of English words with the roots *dog* and *dox*; and the Greek *gignoskein* ("to know"), which is the source of English words with the root *gnos/gnom*.

PRESENT Key Words

(Book D, pages 20–24)

Direct students to read the six root families boldfaced on pages 20–24 of their Level D books. Then have them turn to page 20 to read the boxed key words chorally: *agnostic, amnesty, arraign, criterion, dogma, dogmatic, frenetic, heterodox, hypocrisy, mnemonic, physiognomy, prognosis, rationale, rationalize, schizophrenia.*

Present each key word by discussing the following:

- pronunciation
- definitions/connections to the root
- sentences
- parts of speech
- word forms

Point out the antonyms *heterodox* and *orthodox*. Have students read the prefix definition of *hetero-* ("other," "another," "different") on page 21. Then have them predict what the prefix *ortho-* means, give their reasons, then check their predictions in a dictionary. (*ortho-* means "straight" or "correct.")

Use the *Nota Bene* after *hypocrisy* to discuss the connotation of *cogitate*. Explain that understanding connotation, or shades of meaning, is important if students are to make the most of a thesaurus. Suggest that a student find *cogitate* in a thesaurus and read aloud the list of synonyms. Ask the group for a synonym that is most like *cogitate* in connotation. (Samples: ruminate, deliberate, muse)

GUIDE Practice

Paraphrase Phrases

Have students use their own words to tell what each of these expressions means, then make up examples to illustrate their definitions:

- a *mnemonic* device (Sample: a rhyme, action, or other aid to the memory. Examples: ROY G. BIV for the colors in the spectrum; HOMES for the Great Lakes; FACE for the treble note spaces on a music staff; "I" before "e," except after "c"; "Columbus sailed the ocean blue/In fourteen-hundred ninety-two.")

- language used to *arraign* someone (Sample: words and definitions used in the legal profession. Examples: guilty, innocent, proof)

- symptoms of *schizophrenia* (Sample: signs of this mental illness. Examples: hallucinations, delusions, displaying multiple personalities, talking nonsense, violent behavior)

- people who could grant *amnesty* (Sample: people who could offer pardons. Examples: governors, heads of state, city officials)

- *agnostic* beliefs (Sample: beliefs based on science and reason rather than religion. Examples: there may be either no god, one god, or multiple gods)

- a patient's *prognosis* (Sample: how the patient will fare medically. Examples: full recovery; rehabilitation/physical therapy necessary; surgery will cure the problem; the patient will suffer chronic pain)

- *physiognomy* as an indication of character (Sample: being able to predict what a person is like just by looking at his or her face. Examples: eyes set far apart means tolerant; eyes close together indicates intolerance; crease between the eyes means exacting)

- a *dogmatic* person (Sample: someone who doesn't listen to others' ideas. Examples: a teacher who lectures without taking questions; a political leader who doesn't pay attention to the concerns of his or her constituents; any intolerant person who won't listen to different arguments)

- to *rationalize* one's actions (Sample: coming up with reasons that are just excuses for wrongdoing. Example: Ask students to rationalize stealing some cookies.)

- speaking at a *frenetic* pace (Sample: speaking quickly and without thinking. Example: Ask students to model speaking at a frenetic pace.)

- the *rationale* behind a decision (Sample: why someone does something. Example: Ask students to make up a rationale for not turning in a homework assignment.)

- one *criterion* for graduation (Sample: the courses, grades, passed tests, and other requirements. Ask students: Name one criterion for graduation from our school.)

- a *hypocritical* remark (Sample: a judgment spoken by someone who engages in the same actions they condemn. Example: Ask students to give examples of hypocritical statements and their speakers. ["Honesty is the best policy," spoken by someone who lies; "There's no excuse for rudeness," spoken by someone who talks back to the teacher.])

- to challenge the *dogma* by refusing to give up one's *heterodox* ideas (Sample: to refuse to change your mind even if your ideas are not the accepted way of thinking. Example: Ask students to name some orthodox and heterodox ideas. [orthodox—all students should take the SATs; heterodox—students should be judged only on class participation])

Lesson 3 Key Word Activity Master (see page 117)

Answers:

1. frenetic
2. dogma
3. heterodox
4. dogmatic
5. agnostic
6. mnemonic
7. arraign
8. rationale
9. hypocrisy
10. schizophrenia
11. amnesty
12. rationalize
13. physiognomy
14. prognosis
15. criterion
16. rationalization

ASSIGN Exercises

Book D, pages 24–28

LESSON 4

Literary and Historical References

2. sage   Ralph Waldo Emerson (1803–1882) promoted the philosophy of transcendentalism and the importance of individual moral insight.

William Moulton Marston (1893–1947) combined Greek mythology and Amazon lore to produce the first Wonder Woman comic adventure in 1941.

4. cognizant   Despite criticism of his immoral behavior, Czarina Alexandra (1872–1918) maintained a desperate faith in Grigori Efimovich Rasputin (1871–1916), who claimed healing powers over her hemophiliac son, Aleksei, the heir to the Russian throne.

5. connoisseur   The paintings of Mary Cassatt (1845–1926), an American who studied with the French Impressionists, typically capture domestic scenes. Adelyn Breeskin was director of the Baltimore Museum of Art from 1944 to 1962 and later curator of twentieth-century art at the National Museum of American Art in Washington, D.C.

8. impute   Primarily through the influence of Anytus, whose son had taken to drink when he was forbidden to participate in Socrates' discussions, formal charges were brought against Socrates (469–399 B.C.) for his mode of life and sceptical ideas.

10. putative   Caresse Crosby (Mary Phelps Jacobs) and her maid constructed their prototype of the brassiere from two handkerchiefs and some pink ribbon, and Crosby obtained a patent on the creation in 1914.

11. presage   A historical Welsh leader whom Holinshed's *A Myrroure for Magistrates* describes as a savage, Owen Glendower (1354–1416) appears in Shakespeare's *Henry IV, Part I*, as a poetic scholar whose mystical self-importance irritates his allies.

12. sagacious   Nanyehi (1738–1824), also known as Nancy Ward, was "as famous in war as in the Council." Although she counseled her people to live peacefully, her hopes for good relations with white settlers were dashed in the 1830s when the Cherokee Nation was forced to emigrate to Oklahoma.

13. conscientious Painted by Michelangelo Buonarroti (1475–1564) in the sixteenth century, the famous frescos received a thorough cleaning and restoration in the 1980s.

14. plebiscite Although Corazon Aquino (b. 1933), widow of opposition leader Benigno Aquino, was officially defeated in 1986 by Ferdinand Marcos, she charged that the election had been fraudulent and mounted a campaign of nonviolent resistance that led to Marcos's defeat and exile. A referendum in 1987 affirmed her office as president of the Philippines as well as a new constitution.

Exercise 4B, 1a Spartacus, a Roman slave and gladiator, led an insurrection of Italian slaves known as the Servile Wars in 73 B.C. After routing several Roman armies, Spartacus and his troops were finally defeated in 71 B.C.

Exercise 4B, 2b Ántonia Smerda and the other immigrant farm girls in *My Ántonia* (1918) by Willa Cather (1873–1947) embody the tenacity, fortitude, and resourcefulness of American pioneer women.

Exercise 4B, 3d During the Cultural Revolution Mao Tse-tung (1893–1976) elevated Jiang Qing, his third wife, to the highest level in the Chinese communist party; however, after his death in 1976 she and the other leaders in the radical-left "Gang of Four" were denounced and stripped of power.

Exercise 4B, 4a Born in Russia, Louise Nevelson (1900–1988) became one of America's leading artists of the twentieth century. Using a variety of media from wood to bronze, she combined influences from modern Cubism and Surrealism as well as African, Mayan, and Aztec art.

Exercise 4B, 5d In *The Iliad* Andromache, Hector's wife, pleads with him to withdraw from combat for her sake, but the Trojan hero convinces her that he cannot evade his destiny.

Exercise 4B, 6d Traditional legends of King Arthur tell of a miraculous stone in which a sword is fixed; all the knights try unsuccessfully to remove it, but young Arthur effortlessly slips it out, thus proving his election to the throne.

Exercise 4B, 7a Beginning in 1928, the Grand Ole Op'ry in Nashville, Tennessee, was a successful radio show that featured country music.

Exercise 4B, 7b A member of a pioneer San Francisco family whose fortune was founded by blue jeans manufacturer Levi Strauss, Elise Haas (1894–1990) was herself a painter and sculptor who began collecting art seriously in the late 1940s.

Exercise 4B, 7d   Prized for use in the traditional Japanese tea ceremony, raku ware is typically hand built and fired so as to produce dramatic, unpredictable effects.

Exercise 4B, 9a   On hearing that a ghost has been seen on the battlements, Horatio, the sceptical scholar in Shakespeare's *Hamlet*, delivers a survey of historical ghostly appearances and portents for the listening guards.

Exercise 4B, 9b   The shrine of Dodona, the oldest known Greek oracle, was an oak grove sacred to Zeus; its trees were believed to have the power of speech and prophecy, usually by the means of a priest's interpretation of the rustle of the leaves.

Exercise 4C,   A highly acclaimed Spanish-American writer, Chilean critic and writer Pablo Neruda (1904–1973) is best known for the epic poem "General Song" (1950), biographical writings, and lyric poetry.

Exercise 4C, 3   In Shakespeare's *The Merchant of Venice*, Shylock demands the payment of a pound of Antonio's flesh; Portia, disguised as a judge, rules that Shylock is entitled to the pound but warns that he may not draw a single drop of blood to obtain it.

Exercise 4C, 5   The subtitle of *Tess of the D'Urbervilles* (1891) by Thomas Hardy (1840–1928) reads "A Pure Woman," emphasizing that the outward iniquities of the protagonist's life do not alter the nobility of her character and motives.

Exercise 4C, 7   At its height in the fifteenth century, Inca culture, which extended along the west coast of South America from Colombia through central Chile, was among the most highly developed in the New World, with elaborate irrigation and road systems and fine stonework, all accomplished without the wheel.

Exercise 4C, 10   Irish poet William Butler Yeats (1865–1939) often contrasts the limited perspective of traditional religion and scholarship with the prophetic, mythic vision of the inspired poet.

Exercise 4C, 11   One of the most popular poems of the last century, *The Song of Hiawatha* by Henry Wadsworth Longfellow (1807–1882) evokes a version of Native American life based more on romantic fancy than understanding of native culture.

INTRODUCE Lesson 4

(Book D, page 28)

Remind students that the theme of Lessons 3 and 4 is "Thinking and Knowing."

Display, read, and translate this Latin expression (from page 28 of Lesson 4): *Scire ubi aliquid invenire possis, ea demum maxima pars eruditionis est.* "To know where you can find a thing is in fact the greatest part of learning."

- Have students tell why a reference librarian would agree wholeheartedly with this statement. (Sample: He or she doesn't have to memorize everything if it's possible to retrieve the information.)
- Point to the verb *Scire*, explaining that its meaning "to know" appears in English words with the root *sci*, which are among the words to learn in Lesson 4.

PREVIEW Familiar Words

(Book D, pages 28–31)

notify, recognize, computer, dispute, conscious, science, omniscient

ACTIVITY 1

The Latin *noscere* ("to get to know") and related forms are sources of English words with the root *no/gno/gni*. Help students compare and contrast words with the root.

Display the familiar words *notify* and *recognize*.

Have students use both words in a sentence that tells about knowing. (Samples: You should *notify* the authorities if you *recognize* the suspect./I *recognize* that the *notification* process for college admissions is lengthy, but it is difficult to wait in suspense.)

Point out the *no* in *notify* and the *gni* in *recognize*, explaining that these roots may not look alike but they come from similar Latin words having to do with learning and getting to know. The roots are also related to the Greek *gignoskein*, "to know," which students learned in Lesson 3.

ACTIVITY 2

The Latin *putare* ("to settle," "to consider," "to reckon") and related forms are sources of English words with the root *put*. Help students compare and contrast words with the root.

Display the familiar words *computer* and *dispute.*

Have students name the root that appears in both words. (*put*)

Explain that the words share a Latin root that can mean "to reckon." Reckoning has to do with calculating, considering, analyzing, and figuring out.

Have students tell what the word *computer* has to do with the Latin root meaning "to reckon." (Sample: A *computer* is a machine that can *reckon*, or calculate.)

Ask: What do you think the word *dispute* has to do with the root meaning "to reckon"? (Sample: To *dispute* something is to question whether it is true, so you must *reckon* with the issue, considering it and analyzing it.)

ACTIVITY 3

The Latin *scire* ("to know," "to understand") and related forms are sources of English words with the root *sci*. Help students compare and contrast words with the root.

Display the familiar words *conscious, science, omniscient.*

Read aloud each sentence below with the emphasis shown. Direct students to end the sentence with one of the displayed words:

- Observing and experimenting in order to know about the world are the activities of (science).
- The narrator of a story who knows what all the characters are thinking is said to be (omniscient).
- To know and to be aware is to be (conscious).

Have students name the root that appears in all the words and tell what it means. (*sci* means "to know.")

ACTIVITY 4: Review Familiar Words

Review by having students identify the root in *science, conscious,* and *omniscient (sci)*; *recognize* and *notify (no)*; *computer* and *dispute (put)*. Lesson 4 also includes the Latin *sapere* ("to taste," "to perceive," "to be sensible or wise"), source of English words with the roots *sap/sav*; and *sagire* ("to perceive acutely or keenly with the senses or mind"), the source of English words with the root *sag.*

PRESENT Key Words

(Book D, pages 28–32)

Direct students to read the roots and root families boldfaced on pages 28–31 of their Level D books. Then have them turn to page 28 to read the boxed key words chorally: *cognition, cognizant, compute, connoisseur, conscientious, impute, notorious, plebiscite, presage, prescience, putative, repute, sagacious, sage, sapient.*

Present each key word by discussing the following:

- pronunciation
- definitions/connections to the root
- sentences
- parts of speech
- word forms

Use the *Nota Bene* after *sagacious* to review the origins of the words *sage* (from *sapere*, "to be sensible or wise") and *sagacious* (from *sagire*, "to perceive keenly"). Make the point that even when English words have similar meanings and similar letter clusters—in this case, *sag*—the words may have traveled into English from different starting points and have different connotations.

Use the *Nota Bene* after *conscientious* to discuss the confusables *conscious* and *conscience*. Encourage students to come up with a mnemonic to help them remember the difference (Example: My conscience tells me when to be good [stress the "n" sounds in "conscience" and "when."])

GUIDE Practice

Key Word Q&A

- Would you describe yourself as a *conscientious* worker? Why or why not? (Samples: Yes, I take care in completing my work/No, I just do the minimum to get by.)

- Is it better to be famous or *notorious*? Why? (Sample: It's better to be famous for doing something good than notorious for bad behavior.)

- Have you ever experienced *prescience* before an event? What happened? (Samples: Yes, I once predicted it would snow in May./No, I don't believe we can know the future.)

- Are you a *connoisseur* of something? What is it? (Samples: ice cream, literature, comic book art, watercolor paintings)

- What do you think the best teachers are *sapient* about? (Samples: their students' concerns; the best brands of coffee)

- Do you believe that most people are *cognizant* of their faults? Why do you think that? (Samples: No, most people don't realize their own weaknesses./Yes, most people recognize their faults and either accept them or try to change.)

- How do authors of suspenseful stories *presage* future events? (Samples: use of foreshadowing; presentation of suspicious characters or settings)

- To what might you *impute* the failure of an athlete to live up to expectations? (Samples: too much pressure; bad coaching; too much fame too quickly)

- Is the *putative* inventor of something truly the inventor? Why do you think that? (Sample: Maybe; someone who is reputed to have invented something may or may not have actually done so.)

- What needs to be *computed* during a *plebiscite*? (Sample: votes)

- Would you like to meet someone *reputed* to be a *sage*? Why or why not? (Samples: Yes, I would like to meet a wise person./No, it would make me feel stupid.)

- Is strength in *cognition* usually associated with being *sagacious*? Why do you think that? (Sample: Yes, to be able to perceive or know something involves wisdom./No, someone could be strong in perceiving and knowing but have poor judgment.)

Lesson 4 Key Word Activity Master (see page 118)

Answers:

1. conscientious
2. plebiscite
3. cognition
4. sage
5. impute
6. putative
7. presage
8. notorious
9. cognizant
10. sagacious
11. connoisseur
12. prescience
13. repute
14. sapient
15. two sentences with *compute* (Samples: She used a graphing calculator to *compute* the average./This complicated reading passage does not *compute* with me.)

ASSIGN Exercises

Book D, pages 32–35

REVIEW Lessons 3 and 4

Guide students in creating Hink Pinks that use the key words and word forms in Lessons 3 and 4. Explain that Hink Pinks are a pair of one-syllable rhyming words that answer a silly riddle. Offer one or more examples:

- What do you call a *plebiscite* held by animals related to sheep? (goat vote)
- What are *sapient* males? (wise guys)
- What do you call a *presage* of good things to come? (fine sign)

SELECT Review Exercises

Book D, pages 35–37

LESSON 5

Literary and Historical References

1. alliteration The poetry of American Edna St. Vincent Millay (1892–1950) celebrates Bohemian life, love, and moral freedom.

3. literate Born into a noble Venetian family, Elena Cornaro Piscopia (1646–1684) studied classical and European languages, as well as math, philosophy, astronomy, and theology. Although her disputations attracted scholars from all over Europe and her oral examinations in 1678 had to be held in the Cathedral of Padua to accommodate the crowds, the church objected to a woman's earning a doctorate in theology, and she received instead a doctorate in philosophy.

4. obliterate Two red granite Egyptian obelisks dating from approximately 1500 B.C. first stood in Heliopolis and were moved about 14 B.C. to Alexandria. Both known as Cleopatra's Needle, they now are to be found in London and New York City, where they are subject to damage from air pollution.

5. ascribe This theory was popularized in Professor Martin Bernal's *Black Athena: African and Middle Eastern Roots of Greek Culture,* which contradicts the traditional attribution of Greek civilization to European invaders.

6. circumscribe A world traveler and Buddhist nun, Alexandra David-Neel (1868–1969) was able to penetrate the forbidden territory of Tibet and gain audiences with the Dalai Lama and his family.

8. proscribe Although after World War I the Treaty of Sevres (1920) called for the creation of a new Kurdish state, this new nation never materialized; today the nomadic Kurdish people live in Iran, Iraq, Syria, Turkey, and Armenia, where they are often an abused minority that continues to agitate for a homeland.

9. subscribe The first woman awarded an M.D. degree in the United States, Elizabeth Blackwell (1821–1910) founded the New York Infirmary for Women and Children and its Women's Medical College and helped to establish the London School of Medicine for Women.

10. transcribe   The teachings of Aristotle (384–322 B.C.) were lost to the West after the fall of Rome but flourished in Islamic countries, from which they were reintroduced in the twelfth century by Muslim and Jewish scholars.

13. pseudonym   Harriet Stratemeyer Adams (1894–1982) began writing novels such as the Hardy Boys and the Tom Swift series with her father, Edward Stratemeyer, and extended her efforts to include several popular detective series.

14. ignominious   In *Henry V* Shakespeare contrasts the foppish, arrogant French aristocrats with the battered but goodhearted "happy few" English lads.

Exercise 5B, 1a   Considered China's greatest female poet, Li Ch'ing-chao (1084–1151) was also an art collector, literary critic, history scholar, painter, and political commentator.

Exercise 5B, 1d   When in 1861 her consort, Prince Albert of Saxe-Coburg-Gotha, died suddenly in the prime of life, the bereaved Queen Victoria (1819–1901) retired from public life for several decades.

Exercise 5B, 2a   The Minoans, whose culture developed in Crete and dominated the Mediterranean from about 2000–1000 B.C., were a vigorous maritime people who left evidence of their presence all over the known world.

Exercise 5B, 2b   A continual scandal to British society for his sexual promiscuity, George Gordon, Lord Byron (1788–1824) mocked the moral censure that made him an exile in Italy and Greece in satirical poems such as *Don Juan*, which he began in 1818 and continued writing until his death.

Exercise 5B, 3a   After the death of her husband, Lillian Gilbreth (1878–1972) continued his work as an engineer and efficiency expert. In *Cheaper by the Dozen* her son Frank B. Gilbreth, Jr., describes life in a large family with two geniuses for parents.

Exercise 5B, 4b   Samuel Taylor Coleridge (1772–1834) wrote "The Rime of the Ancient Mariner" at the suggestion of William Wordsworth, and the poem was included in their landmark Romantic volume, *Lyrical Ballads*.

Exercise 5B, 5d   In *A Christmas Carol* (1843) by Charles Dickens (1812–1870), Bob Cratchit is Scrooge's ill-used clerk and the father of Tiny Tim.

Exercise 5B, 7a   Science fiction writer Ray Bradbury (b. 1920) is best known for his social criticism of technology.

Exercise 5B, 7b	In *Great Expectations* (1861) by Charles Dickens (1812–1870), Uncle Pumblechook is the self-important family relation who helps to make Christmas dinner a torment to Pip, the protagonist, and later brings him to Miss Havisham, the local eccentric who changes the boy's life.
Exercise 5B, 8b	Celebrated for her meticulous, ironic poetry, American Marianne Moore (1887–1972) won the Pulitzer Prize and the National Book Award for her *Collected Poems* (1951).
Exercise 5C, 3	These lines appear in "Out, Out—" by Robert Frost (1874–1963).
Exercise 5C, 5	Renaissance painter Jacopo Robusti Tintoretto (1518–1594), taught his daughter, who then worked in his studio. She died young and little work by her hand is known.
Exercise 5C, 6	In *Agamemnon*, the first play of the Oresteian trilogy by Aeschylus (525–456 B.C.), Agamemnon is murdered by his unfaithful wife, Clytemnestra, and her lover, Aegisthus.
Exercise 5C, 7	French writer George Sand (1804–1876) not only adopted a male *nom de plume*, but also shocked society by adopting male dress and smoking cigars, a style that did not prevent her attracting many lovers, including Frederic Chopin.
Exercise 5C, 9	British poet Henry Reed (1914–1986) won fame for his spare, taut poetry about World War II subjects.
Exercise 5C, 10	One of the most renowned singers of her day, Australian soprano Dame Nellie Melba (Helen Mitchell, 1861–1931) inspired the naming of peach Melba and Melba toast.

INTRODUCE Lesson 5

(Book D, page 38)

Tell students that the theme of Lessons 5 and 6 is "Reading and Writing."

Display, read, and translate this Latin expression (from page 38 of Lesson 5): *Nomen est omen.* "A name is an omen."

- Students may know that an omen is a sign. The expression might be restated as "The name reveals everything." It gets at the idea that the meaning of a name influences the holder of the name.
- Ask which Latin word in the expression means "name." *(Nomen)*
- In *Romeo and Juliet*, Romeo asks: "What's in a name? That which we call a rose by any other name would smell as sweet." Ask: Do you agree with this statement, or do you think *Nomen est omen*?
- Tell students that English words with the root *nom* are among the words to learn in Lesson 5.

PREVIEW Familiar Words

(Book D, pages 38–42)

literature, describe, script, antonym, synonym, misnomer, nominate

ACTIVITY 1

The Latin *littera* ("letter") is the source of English words with the root *litera*. Help students think about the root meaning.

Display the familiar word *literature*.

Point out the root *litera*, explaining that it comes from a Latin word meaning "letter."

Ask: What does the familiar word *literature* have to do with the root meaning "letter"? (Samples: Written *literature* is comprised of individual *letters* of the alphabet. *Literature* is often written as fiction, but can also be compiled nonfiction communication or *letters*. *Literature*, learning, writing, and knowledge are sometimes referred to as *"letters"* [for example, the university study of "arts and *letters*"].

ACTIVITY 2

The Latin *scribere* ("to write") and related forms are sources of English words with the root *scrib(e)/script*. Help students compare and contrast words with the root.

Display the familiar words *describe* and *script*.

Read aloud each meaning below with the emphasis shown. Direct students to choose the displayed word that fits:

- to tell about by speaking or writing (describe)
- handwriting (script)
- the written text of a play (script)
- to use a writing implement to trace an outline (describe)

Ask: What is the likely meaning of the Latin root *scribe* or *script*? (having to do with writing) What are some other words about writing that use the root *scribe* or *script*? (Samples: scribe, ascribe, prescribe, description, prescription)

ACTIVITY 3

The Latin *nomen* ("name") is the source of English words with the root *nom/nomen/nomin*. Help students think about the root meaning.

Display the familiar words *misnomer* and *nominate*.

Tell students that the Latin root *nomen* meaning "name" is in both words.

Ask: What kind of *name* is a *misnomer*? (Samples: a mistaken name; a name for a person or place given in error)

Ask: What does *nominating* have to do with *naming*? (Sample: When you *name* someone as a candidate for office, you *nominate* that person.)

ACTIVITY 4: Word Parts

Tell students that the Greek root *onoma* means "name."

Ask students to analyze the words *antonym* and *synonym*, and explain how the word parts work together to give meaning, checking in a dictionary if necessary. (Sample: *Ant(i)-* + *onym* mean "opposite name," and *syn-* + *onym* mean "same or similar name.")

ACTIVITY 5: Review Familiar Words

Review by having students name the root in each displayed familiar word: Latin *littera* ("letter"), Latin *scribere* ("to write"), Greek *onoma* ("name"), Latin *nomen* ("name").

PRESENT Key Words

(Book D, pages 38–42)

Direct students to read the four roots and root families boldfaced on pages 38–42 of their Level D books. Then have them turn to page 38 to read the boxed key words chorally: *acronym, alliteration, ascribe, circumscribe, conscription, ignominious, literal, literate, nomenclature, obliterate, onomatopoeia, proscribe, pseudonym, subscribe, transcribe.*

Present each key word by discussing the following:

- pronunciation
- definitions/connections to the root
- sentences
- parts of speech
- word forms

Point out the antonyms *literate/illiterate*, and have students tell what the prefix *il-* means in these words (not, opposite of). Explain that the prefix *in-* is assimilated, or changes its spelling, to *il-* before the consonant *l*.

Use the *Nota Bene* after *transcribe* to have students identify serif and sans serif typefaces in their books or in a computer font menu. Then ask students to look up *serif* in more than one dictionary in order to explain the word's possible travels into English from the Latin *scribere*.

Use the *Nota Bene* with *nomenclature* to discuss names for recent electronic technologies (Samples: Internet, monitor, hemi [hemispherical engine]). Have students tell which ones they think are based on classical roots and then check their predictions in a dictionary.

GUIDE Practice

For Example

Ask for examples of each of the following:

- words that are *onomatopoeias* (Samples: zoom, zip, whoosh)
- expressions not to be read in a *literal* way (Samples: "in one ear and out the other"; to be "tied up"; "head in the clouds")
- official agencies or organizations that are mainly known by their *acronyms* (Samples: NASA, NATO, UNICEF)
- a synonym for *conscription* (Sample: the draft)
- places where people live in *circumscribed* conditions (Samples: prison, refugee camps, countries where governments prohibit travel)
- *pseudonyms* of famous people (Samples: "Mark Twain" for Samuel Clemens; "Lewis Carroll" for Charles Dodgson; "Maya Angelou" for Marguerite Johnson)
- what people say at *ignominious* moments (Samples: "I'm so ashamed!" "What a humiliating experience!")
- an *alliteration* made with your name (Samples: mild-mannered, modest Matthew; energetic, enthusiastic Elizabeth)
- skills of highly *literate* people (Samples: being able to read, write, and speak well)
- behaviors generally *proscribed* in school (Samples: gum-chewing, violence, intolerance)
- things to *subscribe* to (Samples: viewpoints, magazines, Websites)
- things that are *transcribed* (Samples: music, writings, a recorded interview)
- what successful achievements are often *ascribed* to (Samples: hard work, drive, determination, luck)
- scientific *nomenclature* to identify animals; students may want to use a reference book or the Internet (Samples: *Felis domesticus* for house cat; *Tyrannosaurus rex* for a specific dinosaur; *Canis lupus* for wolf)
- what you'd say after mistakenly *obliterating* your final essay (Samples: "I can't believe I erased my whole paper!" "Maybe my teacher will give me an extension." "My dog ate my homework.")

Lesson 5 Key Word Activity Master (see page 119)

Answers:

1. literal
2. alliteration
3. pseudonym
4. ignominious
5. nomenclature
6. subscribe
7. ascribed
8. onomatopoeia
9. obliterated
10. literate
11. conscripts
12. acronym
13. proscriptions
14. circumscribe
15. transcribed

ASSIGN Exercises

Book D, pages 43–46

LESSON 6

Literary and Historical References

1. epigram   British writer Oscar Wilde (1854–1900) is as well known for his flamboyant lifestyle as for his satirical writing.

3. choreography   Choreographer and director Agnes de Mille (1905–1993) used dance in musical theater to develop character, mood, and plot; her dances incorporated popular forms of American entertainment including tap dancing, jazz, and rodeo rope tricks.

5. graphic   Born a slave, Harriet Ann Jacobs (1813–1897) escaped to the North where she wrote her autobiography, which depicted the sexual exploitation of slave women by their masters.

8. eclectic   Italian physician and educational reformer Maria Montessori (1870– 1952) revolutionized the education of preschool children by introducing "instructive play" that included social, physical, and intellectual skills.

10. analogy   These lines appear in poem XXVII by Emily Dickinson (1830–1886), known also by its first line, "Because I could not stop for Death."

11. apologist   Sarah Winnemucca (1844?–1891) is the author of *Life among the Paiutes: Their Wrongs and Claims* (1883).

12. epilogue   In Shakespeare's 1599 comedy *As You Like It*, the play's protagonist, Rosalind, appears in the epilogue to declare "a good play needs no epilogue."

14. logistics   Napoleon Bonaparte (1769–1821) seems not to have followed his own advice when he let his army become cut off from its supply lines during the Russian campaign.

15. eulogy   In *The Adventures of Tom Sawyer* by Mark Twain (1835–1910) the two friends are presumed drowned but have only been camping out on a Mississippi River island.

Exercise 6B, 2b   In Part II of his "An Essay on Criticism" Alexander Pope (1688–1744) declares: "While from the bounded level of our mind, / Short views we take, nor see the lengths behind; / But more advanced, behold with strange surprise / New distant scenes of endless science rise!"

Exercise 6B, 4b   The only woman famous for painting military subjects, Lady Elizabeth Butler (1850–1933) exhibited at Britain's Royal Academy, but her application for membership was rejected by two votes.

Exercise 6B, 6b	François, sixth Duc de la Rochefoucauld (1613–1680), was a master of the *maxime*, a French literary epigram that expresses a harsh or paradoxical truth with wit and brevity.
Exercise 6B, 6c	English writer Samuel Johnson (1709–1784) cultivated a literary and conversational style of such epigrammatic brilliance that many of his remarks have achieved the status of proverbs.
Exercise 6B, 6d	American satirical poet and short-story writer Dorothy Parker (1893– 1967) was famous in her lifetime for her verbal wit, a talent also reflected in her verse.
Exercise 6B, 8a	A tireless worker for labor reform, women's rights, and temperance, Frances Willard (1839–1898) was a founder of the Women's Christian Temperance Union, the first female head of a women's college, and in 1905 became the first woman whose statue was admitted to the U.S. Capitol.
Exercise 6B, 8b	The temperance movement successfully lobbied for the passage in 1920 of the Eighteenth Amendment to the Constitution, banning sale of alcoholic beverages: however, the rise of bootleggers, "speakeasies," and organized crime around the illegal liquor industry led to the 1933 repeal of Prohibition in the Twenty-first Amendment.
Exercise 6B, 9d	Like Shakespeare, his contemporary, Ben Jonson (1572–1637) wrote comic, historical, and tragic plays.
Exercise 6C, 3	Alabama writer Harper Lee (b. 1926) won the 1960 Pulitzer Prize for her autobiographical novel, *To Kill a Mockingbird.*
Exercise 6C, 4	The preeminent American choreographer of twentieth-century modern dance, Martha Graham (1894–1991) continued to create dances well into her ninth decade.
Exercise 6C, 7	In the epilogue of Shakespeare's *A Midsummer Night's Dream*, Puck, the mischievous elf who attends the fairy king Oberon, appeals for the audience to think of the play as "No more yielding but a dream."
Exercise 6C, 11	English writer Samuel Taylor Coleridge (1772–1834) wrote both poetry and literary criticism; this quotation is a rare combination of the genres.

INTRODUCE Lesson 6

(Book D, page 46)

Remind students that the theme of Lessons 5 and 6 is "Reading and Writing."

Display, read, and translate this Latin quotation (from page 46 of Lesson 6): *Dum lego, assentior.* "While I read, I assent."

- Tell students that the statement was made by Marcus Tullius Cicero, a Roman politician and intellectual famous for his persuasive orations. The quotation expresses Cicero's reaction to reading the ideas of the great Greek philosopher Plato, whose works were written three centuries earlier.

- Ask students whether they have ever "assented" while reading an author's ideas, and to describe the ideas to which they assented.

- Point to *lego*, "I read," explaining that this Latin word is related to Greek words that have furnished the roots *log* and *lex*. These roots are in English words to learn in Lesson 6.

PREVIEW Familiar Words

(Book D, pages 47–49)

autograph, monogram, dialect, dialogue, monologue

ACTIVITY 1

The Greek *graphein* ("scratch," "to draw," "to write") and *gramma* ("picture," letter," "piece of writing") are sources of English words with the roots *graph* and *gram*. Help students think about word parts and root meanings.

Display the familiar words *autograph* and *monogram*.

Have students display both their monogram (a design incorporating their initials) and autograph (signature).

Ask: Which word literally means "self write"? (autograph)

Ask: Which word literally means "single/one write"? (monogram)

What is a meaning for the Greek roots *graph* and *gram*? (write)

ACTIVITY 2

The Greek *lexis* ("speech," "word," "phrase") is the source of English words with the root *lex/lect*. Help students compare and contrast words with the root.

Display the familiar word *dialect*.

Ask: What are some words/pronunciations specific to our region's *dialect*? (Examples: "pop" for "soda" in the Midwest; "bubbler" for "water fountain" in the Northeast; pronunciation of "pen" as "pin" in the South)

Point out the roots *lect* and *lex*, explaining that they appear in words having to do with speech and words.

ACTIVITY 3

The Greek *logos* ("speech," "word," "reason") is the source of English words with the root *log/logue*. Help students compare and contrast words with the root.

Display the familiar words *dialogue* and *monologue*.

Have students tell how a dialogue and a monologue are alike and different. (Sample: Both involve speech. A *dialogue* is a conversation between at least two people; a *monologue* is spoken by one person.)

Ask: What root appears in both words, and what do you think it means? (*logue* means "speech.")

ACTIVITY 4: Word Parts

Have students analyze the displayed familiar words and combine word parts to make a new word. Have them check their new word in a dictionary and tell what it means. (Students may create *monograph*, the name of a written work on a scholarly topic. A less common possibility is *logograph*, which names a kind of written symbol that can be pronounced more than one way.)

ACTIVITY 5: Review Familiar Words

Review by having students identify the root having to do with writing or speech in *dialect (lect)*, *dialogue (logue)*, and *diagram (gram)*.

PRESENT Key Words

(Book D, pages 46–50)

Direct students to read the three roots boldfaced on pages 47–49 of their Level D books. Then have them turn to page 46 to read the boxed key words chorally: *analogy, apologist, choreography, eclectic, epigram, epigraph, epilogue, eulogy, graffiti, graphic, lexicon, lithograph, logistics, logo, topography.*

Present each key word by discussing the following:

- pronunciation
- definitions/connections to the root
- sentences
- parts of speech
- word forms

Use the *Nota Bene* for *anagram* to encourage students to create anagrams of their own names.

Use the *Nota Bene* for *analogy* to discuss why science concepts are sometimes explained through analogy. Students may be able to offer common examples, such as the analogies between a heart and a pump; the eye and a camera.

GUIDE Practice

True or False

Have students hold thumbs up for each true statement and thumbs down for each false statement. Have them use root meanings or definitions to discuss their reasoning, then restate each false statement as a true one:

- An *apologist* is someone who feels ashamed. (False; an apologist is someone who gives *reasons* to support a person or cause.)
- An example of an *epigram* is Mark Twain's comment, "Few things are harder to put up with than the annoyance of a good example." (True; this *witticism* is attributed to Mark Twain.)
- An example of an *epigraph* is a motto inscribed on a building. (True; many buildings display short *writings* or *inscriptions*.)
- Authors use *analogies* to point out secret or hidden differences. (False; an analogy uses *reasoning* to show similarities.)
- The *topography* of islands tends to be alike. (False; island geographies tend to differ dramatically.)
- Pop music performances are usually *choreographed*. (True; most pop musicians hire a professional to create their *dance* moves.)
- A stone statue is an example of a *lithograph*. (False; a lithograph is *printed* material.)
- Advertisers are concerned with *logos*. (True; a logo is a *symbol* that can help quickly identify a product.)
- If a city is famous for its *eclectic* architecture, expect to see variety in building styles. (True; this city would include a blend of architectural styles.)
- Spell-checking software is a *lexicon*. (False; a spell-checker is not a *specialized dictionary*.)
- An *epilogue* could tell what happens to characters after the story ends. (True; an epilogue can appear at the end of a *written* work.)
- A *eulogy* is delivered during a funeral. (True; a eulogy is a *speech* often delivered at a funeral to honor the person who has died.)
- Faulty reasoning is a main concern of the study of *logistics*. (False; logistics studies the *organization of supplies and services*, not logic.)
- A *graphic* designer works mainly with fabrics. (False; he or she works with *print* materials.)
- Computer-generated artwork is an example of *graffiti*. (False; graffiti is found *painted* or *scratched* on walls.)

Lesson 6 Key Word Activity Master (see page 120)

Answers:

1. Yes, a speaker can give a vivid account of an event.
2. Yes, each chapter of *Vocabulary from Classical Roots* begins with an epigraph.
3. No, the members of an orchestra perform music, not dance.
4. Yes, an analogy is a kind of comparison.
5. Yes, a map can show features of topography such as mountains.
6. Yes, an apologist tries to be persuasive and should speak forcefully.

7. No, a logo is a design or picture that might include a name but not a paragraph.

8. No, a state representative is an elected, not eclectic, official.

9. Yes, a lexicon can be a specialized dictionary.

10. No, details are extremely important in the management of supplies and services.

11. No, an epilogue comes at the end of a book or play; a eulogy is a speech of praise, usually at the end of life.

12. Yes, scribblings on a wall could include a witty remark.

13. Yes, a lithographer is a kind of printer, and printing is a graphic art.

ASSIGN Exercises

Book D, pages 50–53

REVIEW Lessons 5 and 6

Have students create 3x3 grids for word puzzles in which the central cell contains a root from Lesson 5 or 6.

- Provide this list of roots: *script, onym, log, graph, gram.*
- Have students choose a root and analyze the key words, familiar words, challenge words, and words in a dictionary in order to list prefixes and suffixes found in the words.
- Guide students in listing the affixes in the cells around the central root so that moving from one cell to a bordering cell results in a real word.
- Have students challenge one another to find and list as many real words as they can for each puzzle. Make defining each listed word a part of the solution.

Sample puzzles:

circum	ive	de
pre	script	con
sub	ion	a

acr	an	pseud
syn	onym	ic
ous	ly	ant

Sample words: circumscription, descriptive, prescription, ascription

Samples words: synonymous, antonymic, pseudonym, acronym

SELECT Review Exercises

Book D, pages 54–55

LESSON 7

Literary and Historical References

1. affable
Goodbye, Mr. Chips, a nostalgic novel about British boarding school life by James Hilton (1900–1954), has become a classic.

2. ineffable
Diane de Poitiers (1499–1566), who became Henry II's mistress while he was still Dauphin, far surpassed the influence of his queen, Catherine de Medici, and was both a patron of and inspiration for the arts.

3. dictatorial
Daphne DuMaurier (1907–1989) based her 1938 novel *Rebecca* on some old letters of her husband and the Cornish estate where she lived.

4. diction
During World War II when radio was the most powerful medium of communication, Franklin Delano Roosevelt (1882–1945) made regular broadcasts to the American public about the progress of the war.

5. dictum
Karl Marx (1818–1883) regarded religion, especially in the form of the established church, as an institution manipulated by the ruling classes to keep the proletariat submissive.

7. edict
Animal Farm by George Orwell (1903–1950) satirizes the authoritarian regime of Russian leader Joseph Stalin.

8. indict
In New Mexico, Grace Newton led a cattle-rustling game that included her sons. History does not record whether Newton ever cleaned up her diction and returned to trial.

9. indite
The Book of Margery Kempe, the life story of an English mystic (1373?– 1440?), provides powerful insights into both spiritual and domestic life of the fifteenth century.

12. malediction
In Shakespeare's *Romeo and Juliet,* Mercutio, who precipitates a fight between members of the feuding Capulet and Montague families, dies cursing both for causing his death.

13. valediction
Dismissed by President Truman as commander during the Korean War because he publicly advocated invading North Korea, World War II general Douglas MacArthur (1880–1964) delivered a moving farewell speech to Congress.

14. gloss
"The Waste Land" (1922) by Thomas Stearns Eliot (1888–1965) consciously draws on the literature of many cultures.

15. polyglot	Mary Antisarlook from Sinruk, Alaska, was hired by Dr. Sheldon Jackson to translate for him on his quest to import Russian reindeer. "Sinruk Mary" was paid for her services in reindeer, and by the early 1900s she was one of the most influential women in the territory, owning one of the largest herds in Alaska.
Exercise 7B, 1b	The works of François Villon (1431–1484?), which mingle bitterness, melancholy, and humor, satirize the establishment of his time.
Exercise 7B, 1d	Maggie Tulliver is the impetuous protagonist of *The Mill on the Floss* by George Eliot (Mary Ann Evans, 1819–1880).
Exercise 7B, 2a	This sonnet by John Keats (1795–1821) describes his delight in discovering Homer, which he first read in George Chapman's translation of *The Iliad*.
Exercise 7B, 3b	His role as "The Sheik" made Rudolph Valentino (1895–1926) the premier "matinee hero" of the silent film era.
Exercise 7B, 4c	The novels and poetry of English writer Thomas Hardy (1840–1928) make frequent use of both classical allusions and Latinate words.
Exercise 7B, 6a	*The Paston Letters*, a collection of correspondence between members of a prosperous Norfolk family, reveal much about domestic life, business matters, social customs, and the law of fifteenth-century England.
Exercise 7B, 6b	Contemporary annotated editions seek to elucidate the many obscure jokes, private allusions, and even mathematical puzzles that Charles Lutwidge Dodgson (1832–1898), better known as Lewis Carroll, embedded in his famous "Alice books."
Exercise 7C, 4	Bernada Alba is the tyrannical mother in *The House of Bernada Alba* by Federico Garcia Lorca (1899–1936).
Exercise 7C, 10	The main streets of central Prague converge at Wencelas Square.

INTRODUCE Lesson 7

(Book D, page 56)

Tell students that the theme of Lessons 7 and 8 is "Speaking."

Display, read, and translate this Latin saying (from page 56 of Lesson 7): *Dictum factum.* "The word is the deed."

- Ask students to compare the meaning of the Latin saying with the English expressions: *As good as one's word* and *Actions speak louder than words.*
- Ask which Latin word in the phrase means "the word." *(Dictum)*
- Tell students that English words with the root *dict* are among the words to learn in Lesson 7.

PREVIEW Familiar Words

(Book D, pages 56–59)

infant, dictate, dictionary, predict, glossary

ACTIVITY 1

The Latin *fari* ("to speak," "to confess," "to admit") and related forms are sources of English words with the root *fan/fa(t)*. Help students think about the root meaning.

Display the familiar word *infant*, and ask for a definition. (a very young child)

Tell students that the second syllable of *infant* comes from a Latin word meaning "to speak."

Ask: What does the Latin root meaning "to speak" have to do with the meaning of *infant*? (Sample: An *infant* is not yet able to *speak*.) Remind students that the prefix *in-* can mean "not."

ACTIVITY 2

The Latin *dicere* ("to say," "to tell") and related forms are sources of English words with the root *dict*. Help students compare and contrast words with the root.

Display the familiar words *dictate, dictionary,* and *predict.*

Read aloud each of these sentences with the emphasis shown. Direct students to end the sentence with one of the displayed words:

- When you say words for others to write down, you (dictate).
- To say what will happen before it happens is to (predict).
- When you want to say words properly, use a (dictionary).

Ask: What is a meaning of the root *dict*? (say)

ACTIVITY 3

The Greek *glossa* ("tongue," "language") and related forms are sources of English words with the root *gloss/glot*. Help students think about the root meaning.

Display the familiar word *glossary*.

Have students tell what a glossary is and explain its purpose. (A glossary is a list of special terms and definitions that usually appears in the back of a book.)

Point out that the root *gloss* appears in English words having to do with language or foreign terms.

ACTIVITY 4: Multiple Meanings

Ask students to explain the meaning differences of *dictate* in these sentences:

- I will *dictate* sentences for students to write.
- I try to follow the *dictates* I believe in.

Have a student read aloud the dictionary definitions of *dictate* as listeners decide which meaning fits each context.

ACTIVITY 5: Review Familiar Words

Review by having students give a meaning for the Lesson 7 roots *fan(t)* ("speak," "tell," "confess"), *dict* ("say," "tell"), and *gloss* ("language").

PRESENT Key Words

(Book D, pages 56–60)

Direct students to read the three root families boldfaced on pages 56–59 of their Level D books. Then have them turn to page 56 to read the boxed key words chorally: *affable, dictatorial, diction, dictum, ditty, edict, gloss, indict, indite, ineffable, interdiction, jurisdiction, malediction, polyglot, valediction.*

Present each key word by discussing the following:

- pronunciation
- definitions/connections to the root
- sentences
- parts of speech
- word forms

Use the *Nota Bene* after *indite* to have students summarize the meaning difference between homonyms *indict* and *indite* (Sample: *indict* means "to issue a formal charge of a crime"; *indite* means "to write or compose." Emphasize that using the scholarly word *indite* as a synonym for *write* or *compose* is likely to sound artificial, so students should only use it within the context of academic works.

Use the *Nota Bene* after *valediction* to have students summarize the connotative difference between *edict* and *dictum*. (Sample: An *edict* is an overarching official ruling; a *dictum* is only as official as the person expressing it.)

Point out the antonyms *malediction* and *benediction*, and have students predict what the prefixes *bene-* and *male-* mean, give their reasons, then check their predictions in a dictionary. (*Bene-* means "good," "well"; *mal(e)-* means "bad.")

GUIDE Practice

Categories

Have students name the key word or words that belong in each list, and tell what the words have in common:

- index, footnote, heading, (gloss; all are features of an informational text)
- eulogy, oration, lecture, (valediction; all are speeches)
- prohibition, ban, proscription, (interdiction; all are synonyms for rules against certain activities)
- friendly, encouraging, warm, (affable; all describe a person who is easy to be with)
- nursery rhyme, advertising jingle, limerick, (ditty; all name short and rhythmical lines that are spoken or sung)
- curse, denunciation, execration, (malediction; all are expressions of ill wishes against someone or something)
- scholar, Renaissance man or woman, jack-of-all-trades (polyglot; all are people with broad knowledge)
- compose, draft, revise, (indite; all have to do with writing)
- accuse, arraign, try, (indict; all have to do with bringing a person to trial for allegedly committing a crime)
- government, authority, protectorship, (jurisdiction; all have to do with taking charge of people or places)
- controlling, autocratic, bossy, (dictatorial; all describe leaders who expect complete obedience)
- wondrous, awe-inspiring, astonishing, (ineffable; all indicate powerful experiences that are difficult to describe)
- drawl, dialect, intonation, (diction; all have to do with ways of saying words and sentences)
- proclamation, judgment, decree, (edict, dictum; all name authoritative orders)

Lesson 7 Key Word Activity Master (see page 121)

Answers:

1. edict
2. dictatorial
3. indite
4. ditty
5. jurisdiction
6. affable
7. valediction
8. interdiction
9. indict
10. dictum
11. diction
12. polyglot
13. ineffable
14. gloss
15. malediction
16. contradictions

ASSIGN Exercises

Book D, pages 60–63

LESSON 8

Literary and Historical References

1. acclamation   Shirley Chisholm (b. 1924) represented the predominantly black Bedford-Stuyvesant district of New York in the U.S. Congress.

Written in 1876 by Henry Martyn (1837–1923), *Robert's Rules of Order* is the standard authority on parliamentary procedure in the United States.

2. clamor   These lines are from "The Poets" by American poet Henry Wadsworth Longfellow (1807–1882).

The style and blond beauty of German-American film actress Marlene Dietrich (1901–1992) influenced a generation of American and European women in the 1930s and 1940s.

3. declaim   Hoping to make serious music more accessible to popular audiences, American composer Aaron Copland (1900–1991) wrote a number of works such as *A Lincoln Portrait* (1942) using American themes and folk tunes.

4. forensic   Daughter of Zulfikar Ali Bhutto, the former prime minister of Pakistan, and herself prime minister from 1988 to 1991, Benazir Bhutto (b. 1953) was the first woman elected to head the government in an Islamic country.

6. lingo   A novel of violent youth in a sterile future society, *A Clockwork Orange* by Anthony Burgess (1917–1993) exemplifies the author's satirical criticism of contemporary life.

12. loquacious   In *Oedipus Rex* by Sophocles (496?–406 B.C.), the chatty messenger who was sent to announce that Oedipus is the new king of Corinth continues his narrative in hopes of further ingratiating himself with the ruler and thus reveals that Oedipus was an adopted child.

Exercise 8B, 2c   A slave captured in European wars, Roxelana (also known as Haseki Hurrem, "the joyous favorite") became the principal wife of Suleiman the Magnificent (1495?–1566).

Exercise 8B, 3b   Mrs. Bennet's continual promotion of her marriageable daughters provides much of the humor of *Pride and Prejudice* by Jane Austen (1775–1817).

Exercise 8B, 3c   Father Brown is the unlikely detective created by British writer G. K. Chesterton (1874–1936).

Exercise 8B, 5a	Although she spent much of her life in the United States, novelist Marguerite Yourcenar (1903–1987) wrote only in French.
Exercise 8B, 5b	Aretha Franklin (b. 1942) has made more records selling over a million copies than any woman in the history of recorded sound.
Exercise 8B, 5c	President Richard Nixon (1913–1994) was forced to resign from office in 1974 under threat of impeachment.
Exercise 8B, 5d	*The Tale of Genji* by Japanese courtier Murasaki Shikibu (978?–1031?) is considered the first example of the novel in any culture.
Exercise 8B, 6a	In 1897 Jack London (1876–1916) joined the rush to the Klondike goldfields, an experience that never made him rich but provided a lifetime of adventures to write about in his stories and novels.
Exercise 8B, 6c	Charlene Hunter Gault (b. 1942) is now a television journalist.
Exercise 8B, 7d	Jakob Grimm (1785–1863) also collected European folktales.
Exercise 8C, 9	Scholars distinguish three general periods in the development of the English language: Old English ca. 450–1150, exemplified by *Beowulf*; Middle English, 1150–1550, exemplified by the works of Chaucer; Modern English, 1550–present.

INTRODUCE Lesson 8

(Book D, page 63)

Remind students that the theme of Lessons 7 and 8 is "Speaking."

Display, read, and translate this Latin saying (from page 63 of Lesson 8): *Verbum sat sapienti.* "A word to a wise person is enough."

- Ask whether students have ever heard the expression "A word to the wise," "A word for the wise," or "A word to the wise is enough," and discuss meaning. (Sample: A wise person needs few words to understand something.)
- Point to the Latin word *Verbum*, explaining that its meaning—"word"— appears in English words with the root *verb*, which are among the words to learn in Lesson 8.

PREVIEW Familiar Words
(Book D, pages 64–67)

exclaim, proclaim, bilingual, linguistic, eloquent, proverb, verb

ACTIVITY 1

The Latin *clamare* ("to cry out," "to shout") and related forms are sources of English words with the root *clam/claim*. Help students compare and contrast words with the root.

Display the familiar words *exclaim* and *proclaim*.

Have students identify the shared root in both words *(claim)*.

Have students say each quoted statement as described:

- "I am the winner!" (s)he exclaimed.
- "I am the winner!" (s)he proclaimed.

Ask students how *exclaiming* and *proclaiming* are alike and how they differ. (Sample: Both are ways of using the voice and expressing ideas. When you *exclaim*, you cry out in surprise. When you *proclaim*, you make an announcement.)

Tell students that the root *claim* comes from a Latin word meaning "to cry out."

ACTIVITY 2

The Latin *lingua* ("speech," "language," "tongue") is the source of English words with the root *ling(u)*. Help students compare and contrast words with the root.

Display the familiar words *bilingual* and *linguistic*.

Have students name the root that appears in both words *(lingu)* and tell what each word has to do with the Latin root meaning "language." (A speaker of two languages is *bilingual*; the adjective *linguistic* means "having to do with language.")

ACTIVITY 3

The Latin *loqui* ("to speak") and related forms are sources of English words with the root *loqu/loc*. Help students think about the root meaning.

Display the familiar word *eloquent*.

Point out the root *loqu*, explaining that it comes from a Latin word meaning "to speak."

Ask students to describe an eloquent speaker. (Samples: persuasive, powerful, emotional, effective)

ACTIVITY 4

The Latin *verbum* ("word") is the source of English words with the root *verb*. Help students think about word parts and root meaning.

Display the familiar words *proverb* and *verb*.

Tell students that the English word *verb*, which names a part of speech, is also a root that comes from a Latin word meaning "word."

Ask: What word parts are in *proverb*? (the prefix *pro-* and the root *verb*).

Point out that the prefix *pro-* in *proverb* means "forth"; the root *verb* means "word."

Ask how those meanings combine in *proverb*. (Sample: A *word*, or comment, is put *forth* in a *proverb*, which is a short saying that gets at a basic truth.)

Have students name some proverbs (Samples: A fool and his money are soon parted./Beauty is skin deep./History repeats itself.)

ACTIVITY 5: Root Meanings

Have students use each displayed familiar word in an oral sentence that offers strong hints at the root meaning. (Sample: *The bilingual linguist eloquently exclaimed, "I do proclaim, that proverb is missing its verb!"*)

ACTIVITY 6: Review Familiar Words

Review by having students identify the root in *proclaim* and *exclaim* (*claim*, Latin "to cry out"); *bilingual* and *linguistic* (*lingu*, Latin "speech," "language"); *eloquent* (*loqu*, Latin "speak"); *verb* and *proverb* (*verb*, Latin "word"). Lesson 8 also includes the Latin *forum* ("forum," "place out of doors").

PRESENT Key Words

(Book D, pages 63–67)

Direct students to read the roots and root families boldfaced on pages 64–67 of their Level D books. Then have them turn to page 63 to read the boxed key words chorally: *acclamation, circumlocution, clamor, colloquium, declaim, forensic, forum, lingo, lingua franca, linguist, locution, loquacious, proverbial, verbatim, verbose.*

Present each key word by discussing the following:

- pronunciation
- definitions/connections to the root
- sentences
- parts of speech
- word forms

Use the *Nota Bene* after *forum* to ask how the meanings of *forensics* and *forum* are related. (Sample: A *forum* is a public meeting where debating, or *forensics*, may occur.)

Use the *Nota Bene* after *linguist* to ask students to review *polyglot* in Lesson 7 and tell the main difference between the origins of the synonyms *linguist* and *polyglot*. (The word *linguist* has the Latin root *lingua* meaning "tongue," and the word *polyglot* has a Greek root *glot* meaning "tongue.")

Use the *Nota Bene* after *verbose* to have students offer oral sentences to show the meaning and usage differences between *verbose* and *loquacious* (Sample: A *loquacious* speaker may not be *verbose* in his or her writing.)

GUIDE Practice

Synonyms

Have students name the key word or words that belong in each list of words with similar meanings:

- famous, widespread, notorious,   (proverbial)
- grammarian, lexicographer, etymologist,   (linguist)
- evasion, indirection, roundaboutness,   (circumlocution)
- approval, applause, favor,   (acclamation)
- insist, demand, cry out,   (clamor)
- speechify, recite, orate,   (declaim)
- expression, phrase, saying,   (locution)
- word-for-word, exact, letter-perfect,   (verbatim)
- debate, argumentation, rhetoric,   (forensic)
- meeting, gathering, assembly,   (forum, colloquium)
- talkative, garrulous, long-winded,   (loquacious, verbose)
- jargon, trade language, slang,   (lingo, lingua franca)

Lesson 8 Key Word Activity Master (see page 122)

Answers:

1. verbatim
2. lingua franca
3. proverbial
4. loquacious
5. declaim
6. lingo
7. locution
8. forensic

9. clamor

10. linguist

11. colloquium

12. verbose

13. circumlocution

14. forum

15. two sentences with *acclamation* (Samples: The famous Broadway star was greeted with *acclamation.*/The class voted in *acclamation*, agreeing to start a classroom recycling program.

ASSIGN Exercises

Book D, pages 67–71

REVIEW Lessons 7 and 8

Because the words in these lessons are about speaking, many lend themselves to dramatic interpretation. Have small groups develop skits in which actors show the meaning of phrases such as these:

- precise diction
- a pedantic circumlocution
- a loquacious guest
- acclamation from the crowd
- a dictatorial manner
- a Shakespearean malediction
- a ridiculous ditty
- an affable greeting

After each brief performance, audience members try to guess what is being demonstrated.

SELECT Review Exercises

Book D, pages 71–73

LESSON 9

Literary and Historical References

NOTA BENE: Part One of Book D focuses on properties of the mind: thought and language. Part Two moves into the cosmos with components of the universe, including earth, air, fire, and water, a traditional foursome having a scientific and medical history that goes back to ancient times.

In the sixth century B.C., religious and philosophical inquiry led Greek thinkers to identify, in succession, water, fire, air, and earth as the four basic elements of the universe. Empedocles, a renowned physician in the fifth century B.C., recognized the function of these elements as opposites: hot (fire) and cold (air), wet (water) and dry (earth). He also believed that two opposing forces he called "love" and "strife" could increase or disturb the harmony of the four basic elements.

Another influential physician, Galen, in the second century A.D., saw a correspondence between the four elements and four fluids in the human body: air and blood, water and phlegm or mucus, earth and black bile, and fire and yellow bile. By the Middle Ages these relationships dictated medical diagnosis according to a formal system known as *humoralism,* based on the Latin *humor,* meaning "moisture." Humors dictated a person's disposition and state of health. A large supply of blood (hot and wet) caused a person to be *sanguine,* or cheerful, while an excess of phlegm (cold and wet) made a person *phlegmatic,* or listless. A preponderance of black bile or gall (cold and dry) made one *melancholy,* and yellow bile from the liver (hot and dry) created a *choleric* temperament, or irritability. An even—or harmonious—distribution of the four humors meant a pleasant disposition and good digestion. Imbalance of humors required that a patient be bled or purged, often with results more harmful than curative.

For centuries the humors of literary characters were visible in their behavior. Readers of *The Canterbury Tales* recall the sanguine, ruddy-faced Franklin always ready for guests at his table and the choleric Reeve, a devious steward, feared by his underlings. Shakespeare's audiences could attribute part of Hamlet's melancholy to a superfluity of black bile. The phlegmatic philosopher Jacques in *As You Like It* could be world-weary because of an excess of phlegm. Sometimes writers treated humors lightly, as did playwright Ben Jonson in *Every Man in his Humour* and *Every Man out of his Humour,* the latter called a "Comicall Satyre." By the eighteenth century the word *humor* had acquired the meaning of "something amusing" as we know it.

The rise of the scientific method during the period of Enlightenment in the eighteenth century began to displace faith in humoralism, which was not thoroughly discredited until well into the nineteenth century. Its vocabulary, however, is still current today.

1. apogee   Published in 1936, *Gone with the Wind* became a best-seller for American novelist Margaret Mitchell (1900–1949).

2. geocentric

Greek astronomers may have determined the principle of heliocentrism as early as the fourth century B.C., but Aristarchus was the first to give a full account of it in writing.

3. perigee

Unlike *apogee, perigee* is not used metaphorically.

4. inter

In Shakespeare's play *Julius Caesar* (1600–1601) Mark Antony seems to praise Brutus for his part in the slaying of Caesar and to condemn the slain emperor, but his funeral oration actually stirs the crowd to believe in Caesar's wrongful murder.

6. terrestrial

English poet Thomas Hardy (1840–1928), on the bleak last day of the year 1900, finds hope for the new century in the unexpected song of a bird.

7. exhume

Using exhumed bodies for study required secrecy; a trap door in the dissection room allowed a body to be slipped into the river below when unauthorized persons appeared.

The earliest known draft of *The Adventures of Huckleberry Finn* in Mark Twain's own hand turned up in 1991.

8. humus

An authority on gardens, British author Victoria Sackville-West (1892– 1962) for fourteen years wrote a column about gardening for the London *Observer.*

9. mountebank

At first a collector of oddities, American showman Phineas Taylor Barnum (1810–1891) gained credibility when he sponsored genuinely talented performers, notably Swedish soprano Jenny Lind.

11. promontory

In the Greek myth, Theseus has saved himself and thirteen other youths by slaying the Minotaur, but on his return he forgets to substitute the agreed-upon white sail for the black one.

12. pastoral

English novelist Anthony Trollope (1815–1882) wrote about relationships in families, business, politics, and religion.

The extravagance of Marie Antoinette (1755–1793) in pursuit of pastoral and other pleasures contributed to discontent among French revolutionaries, who set the stage for the execution of King Louis XVI in 1793 and that of the queen nine months later.

14. rustic

Rustic figures in the novels of Thomas Hardy (1840–1928) not only provide a social record of agricultural England but also embody a lost rural simplicity.

15. rusticate

During the Cultural Revolution (1966–1969) the social and economic reforms of Chairman Mao Tse-tung emphasized dispersal of professional people to the countryside.

Exercise 9B, 1a One of the most skillful military leaders in history, Alexander the Great (356–323 B.C.) subjugated Greece, Egypt, India, Pakistan, Afghanistan, Iran, and Turkey.

Exercise 9B, 1b After losing a poetry competition, renowned poet of the Tang Dynasty, Tu Fu (712–770), rode for thirty years through the countryside on a donkey, deepening his understanding of political and social upheavals of the time.

Exercise 9B, 2a In *One Generation After* (1965) Romanian-born author Elie Wiesel (b. 1928) tells of his return to his native village. He describes deportation and concentration camp experiences in his autobiographical *Night*.

Exercise 9B, 2b Manuscripts unearthed from trunks in Scotland and Ireland in the 1920s provided the first full portrait of Scottish author James Boswell (1740– 1795), until then known primarily as the assiduous biographer of Samuel Johnson.

Exercise 9B, 3b In *The Little Prince* (1943) French author Antoine de Saint-Exupéry (1900–1944) expresses the faith in life and human beings that he demonstrated as an aviator and writer about World War II flying missions.

Exercise 9B, 4a As portrayed in Sophocles' play *Antigone*, that character defies her uncle Creon, clawing a grave for the brother who has been denied formal burial for disloyalty to the state.

Exercise 9B, 4d *Wuthering Heights* by Emily Brontë (1818–1848) received recognition as a masterpiece only after the author's death.

Exercise 9B, 5a American author Harriette Arnow (1908–1986) is best known for the novels *The Dollmaker* (1954) and *The Weedkiller's Daughter* (1970).

Exercise 9B, 5b Through period buildings, original artifacts, and live demonstrations, Old Sturbridge Village, located in southern Massachusetts, replicates the way of life in America from 1790 to 1840.

Exercise 9B, 5d Appearing on television from 1962 to 1971, *The Beverly Hillbillies* was a comedy about the Clampett family.

Exercise 9B, 6a King Beowulf of the Geats, thought to have lived in the eighth century, is the hero of the first epic in English (Anglo-Saxon).

Exercise 9B, 7a Polish astronomer Nicolaus Copernicus (1473–1543) upset orthodox beliefs in geocentrism, and by means of an improved telescope Galileo Galilei (1564–1642) verified heliocentrism, in the process inciting defamation by the Inquisition in 1616.

Exercise 9B, 7b	Devising adventures that anticipated later scientific achievements, French novelist Jules Verne (1828–1905) is the author of *Journey to the Center of the Earth* (1864).
Exercise 9B, 8b	In *O Pioneers!* Willa Cather (1873–1947) presents the struggles of nineteenth-century immigrants in Nebraska.
Exercise 9B, 8c	In his "Recollections of Life in the Country," German composer Ludwig von Beethoven (1770–1827) describes the theme of his 1808 *Pastoral* Symphony as a hymm to nature.
Exercise 9B, 8d	A professor of philosophy and medieval studies, American author Ralph McInerny (b. 1929) is also the creator of Father Dowling, a Catholic priest and amateur detective.
Exercise 9C, 1	American Harry Houdini (1874–1926), born Ehrich Weiss, was such an accomplished magician and escape artist that he could detect mountebanks and expose them effectively.
Exercise 9C, 2	Defying family protests against political involvement, Doña Felisa Rincón de Gautier (b. 1897) helped found the Popular Party in Puerto Rico and in 1946 became the first mayor of San Juan, a post she held for twenty-two years.
Exercise 9C, 3	*Anecdotes of Destiny* by Danish author Isak Dinesen (Baroness Karen Blixen, 1885–1962) contains the story "Babette's Feast."
Exercise 9C, 5	In the *Decameron*, Italian author Giovanni Boccaccio (1313–1375) tells 100 stories, a tale a day for ten days by each of ten young Florentines entertaining themselves while avoiding the Black Death raging in the city.
Exercise 9C, 9	Since 1974 when farmers first discovered terra cotta fragments in Xi'an, China, archaeologists have unearthed and reassembled figures of soldiers, horses, and carts of the funerary escort ordered by the first emperor of the Qin dynasty (221 B.C.–206 B.C.).

INTRODUCE Lesson 9

(Book D, page 77)

Tell students that the theme of Lessons 9 and 10 is "Earth and Air."

Display, read, and translate this Latin term (from page 77 of Lesson 9): *Terra firma.* "Solid ground."

Tell students that English-speakers use *terra firma* in statements such as this one: "What a relief to be on terra firma again!" Discuss the situations that might provoke that remark. (Samples: disembarking from a ship or roller coaster)

Ask: Which Latin word means "ground"? *(terra)* Explain that English words with the root *terr* are among the words to learn in Lesson 9.

PREVIEW Familiar Words

(Book D, pages 78–81)

geography, geology, terrain, humble, amount, mountain, rural

ACTIVITY 1

The Greek *gaia* ("the earth") is the source of English words with the root *geo/gee*. Help students compare and contrast words with the root.

Display the familiar words *geography* and *geology*.

Ask: What root is in both words? *(geo)*

Ask: What is the difference in meaning between *geography* and *geology*, and how are they similar? (Sample: *Geography* is the study of the landforms, waters, peoples, and weather of the earth. *Geology* is the science of rocks, minerals, and layers of planet Earth. Both are sciences having to do with the earth.)

Ask: What does the root *geo* mean? ("earth")

ACTIVITY 2.

The Latin *terra* ("earth," "land," "ground") is a source of English words with the root *ter(r)*. Help students think about the root meaning.

Display the familiar word *terrain*.

Have students tell how rugged terrain is different from flat terrain, and where you might see each one. (Sample: Rugged terrain is ground that is hilly and rocky, like in the woods. Flat terrain is level ground, like on a paved highway.)

Point out the root *terr*, explaining that it may be part of English words having to do with earth or land.

ACTIVITY 3

The Latin *humus* ("earth") is the source of English words with the root *hum*. Help students understand that other meanings have grown from the root.

Display the familiar word *humble*.

Have students demonstrate humble actions and their opposites. (Samples: a humble bow, a humble smile, a humble handshake)

Explain that the root *hum* in *humble* comes from a Latin word for "earth." Ask for students' ideas about the connection between the Latin root and the English word. Then ask a student to read aloud the dictionary derivation of *humble*. Discuss how the root meaning of "ground" is connected to lowly people, places, or things.

ACTIVITY 4

The Latin *mons* ("mountain") and related forms are sources of English words with the root *mont/mount*. Help students understand that other meanings have grown from the root.

Display the familiar words *amount* and *mountain*.

Ask for students' ideas about how the words *amount* and *mountain* are alike in meaning.

Ask a student to read aloud the dictionary derivation of *amount*. Discuss how the root meaning is connected to modern meanings. (Students will find that the root meaning has to do with climbing a mountain; that idea extended to reaching higher "amounts" by adding up numbers or quantities.)

ACTIVITY 5

The Latin *rus* ("open land," "country") and related forms are sources of English words with the root *rur/rus*. Help students think about the root meaning.

Display the familiar word *rural*.

Tell students that the word *rural* includes the root *rur* that comes from a Latin word for "country."

Ask students to describe a rural setting (they should automatically use the word *country* in their descriptions).

ACTIVITY 6: Description

Ask students to describe the local *terrain*, using at least one of the displayed words in their description.

ACTIVITY 7: Review Familiar Words

Review by having students give a meaning for the Lesson 9 roots that appear in "terrain" (Latin *terra*, "earth"); "mountain" (Latin *mons*, "mountain"); "geography" (Greek *gaia*, "the earth"); "rural" (Latin *ruris*, "open land," "country"); and "humble" (Latin *humus*, "earth"). Lesson 9 also includes the Latin *pascere* ("to feed") and *pastor* ("shepherd"), which are sources of English words with the root *past*.

PRESENT Key Words

(Book D, pages 77–82)

Direct students to read the six roots and root families boldfaced on pages 78–81 of their Level D books. Then have them turn to page 77 to read the boxed key words chorally: *apogee, exhume, geocentric, humus, inter, mountebank, paramount, pastoral, perigee, promontory, repast, rustic, rusticate, terra cotta, terrestrial.*

Present each key word by discussing the following:

- pronunciation
- definitions/connections to the root
- sentences
- parts of speech
- word forms

Point out that *apogee* and *perigee* are antonyms. Ask students to think of a mnemonic device for remembering the difference. (Sample: *apogee* means *acme* or *apex*—the highest point)

Ask students if they have ever eaten *humus* (more commonly, *hummus*): "a paste of pureed chickpeas usually mixed with sesame oil or sesame paste and eaten as a dip or sandwich spread." This meaning is from the Arabic for "chickpea." Point out that the food looks like "rich, dark organic material formed by decay of vegetable matter, essential to soil's fertility" to make a possible meaning connection across languages and cultures. Ask students if they can think of other foods named for what they look like (Sample: pigs in a blanket, lady fingers, cabbage [means "head" in Old French], vermicelli [means "little worms" in Italian]).

Point out the antonyms for *inter: disinter* and *exhume*. Have students use all three words as they explain opposing and similar meanings. (Sample: After the corpse was *interred*, the body was *exhumed* and the foul play was *disinterred*, or presented to the public.) Contrast the pronunciation and meaning of the verb *inter* ("to bury") with the prefix *inter-* (prefix means "between, among").

Point out the antonyms *terrestrial, celestial,* and *aquatic.* Have students name a terrestrial being, a celestial body, and an aquatic animal (Samples: humans, the sun, a fish).

Use the *Nota Bene* after *rusticate* to make the point that English has abundant synonyms largely because of the different languages contributing words at different times as the English language evolves.

GUIDE Practice

Cause and Effect

Have students complete each sentence:

- Avoid medical treatment from a *mountebank* because (Sample: a mountebank is a charlatan and is offering fake cures.)

- Sometimes a body must be *exhumed* because (Sample: it is needed for a criminal investigation.)

- *Terra cotta* has practical value because (Sample: it can be made into pots for cooking and holding plants.)

- Earth's moon reaches a *perigee* because (Sample: the shape of the moon's orbit means that there is a point at which it is closest to Earth.)

- Wheeled vehicles are *terrestrial* because (Sample: they don't work in water or in the air.)

- People look forward to a *repast* when (Sample: they are very hungry.)

- Shelter is a *paramount* need because (Sample: protection from the elements is essential to human survival.)

- Gardeners need *humus* because (Sample: it enriches the soil.)

- City dwellers may choose to *rusticate* because (Sample: they enjoy the fresh air and scenery of the country.)

- Someone at the *apogee* of a profession is probably skillful because (Sample: to be at the peak of a profession usually means that the person has skills that come from experience.)

- A *geocentric* theory of the solar system is unacceptable because (Sample: the sun, not planet Earth, is at the center of the solar system.)

- An artist might decide to paint a *pastoral* landscape because (Sample: it would have an appealing peaceful and restful mood.)

- Pharaohs were *interred* with their riches because (Sample: the ancient Egyptians believed that riches could be used in the afterlife.)

- A *promontory* is a good place for an ocean view because (Sample: it juts out high over the water.)

- A *rustic* life is challenging because (Sample: you have few luxuries and must live off the land.)

Lesson 9 Key Word Activity Master (see page 123)

Answers:

1. terra cotta
2. pastoral
3. interment
4. rustic
5. mountebank
6. perigee
7. humus
8. rusticate
9. terrestrial
10. paramount
11. apogee
12. repast
13. geocentric
14. promontory
15. exhumed
16. MEDITERRANEAN (S)EA

ASSIGN Exercises

Book D, pages 82–86

LESSON 10

Literary and Historical References

1. animus
With the title *Moby-Dick*, American novelist Herman Melville (1819–1891) emphasizes the importance of the whale pursued so monomaniacally.

1. animus
Without sight or hearing after an illness at age two, Helen Keller (1880–1968) escaped from her silent world with the help of her teacher Anne Sullivan (1866–1936), who herself suffered from impaired vision.

3. pusillanimous
In *The Wizard of Oz* American author Frank Baum (1856–1919) introduced not only the Cowardly Lion, but also other characters who appear in the series of fourteen Oz books.

4. ether
First used in the 1840s, ether and chloroform released women from pain in childbirth, and Queen Victoria's use of the latter helped remove guilt for avoiding the pain promised Eve, according to Genesis.

5. ethereal
The well-known ballet *The Nutcracker* by Pĕtr Ilich Tchaikovsky (1840–1893) is often performed during the Christmas season.

English poet William Wordsworth (1770–1850) concludes the poem by saying that although the skylark is ethereal, it is "True to the kindred points of Heaven and Home."

6. diaphanous
Flamboyant and innovative, American dancer Isadora Duncan (1878– 1927) toured successfully in Europe and influenced modern dance through schools she founded.

7. epiphany
The story of Jacob can be found in Genesis 32:24-29.

With strains of the song "John Brown's Body" lingering in her head after she attended a military review in 1861, abolitionist, suffragist, and poet Julia Ward Howe (1819–1910) woke in the middle of the night, inspired to write new words to the melody that became "The Battle Hymn of the Republic."

9. sycophant
Flattering courtiers inflate King Richard II's belief in his divine right, which leads him to overspend and mishandle political alliances in Shakespeare's play *Richard II* (1595–1597).

10. aspiration   The founder of the National Political Congress of Black Women, Shirley Chisholm (b. 1924) is the first black woman to have been elected to the U.S. Congress, where she served seven terms.

In the play *Pygmalion* by English dramatist George Bernard Shaw (1856–1950), Professor Henry Higgins transforms an uneducated Cockney flower seller into a convincing English lady by teaching her how to speak properly.

Exercise 10B, 1a   American composer Scott Joplin (1868–1917) suffered a major disappointment when his folk opera *Treemonisha* received an indifferent response from critics. The use of one of his ragtime compositions in the 1973 film *The Sting* revived interest in his music.

Exercise 10B, 1d   Mae C. Jemison was a 1981 medical school graduate before being selected in 1987 for training as an astronaut in the U.S. space program.

Exercise 10B, 2b   Russian choreographer Michel Fokine (1880–1942) transformed ballet from stiff tableaux to dramatic movements and created *The Dying Swan* for Anna Pavlova (1885–1931), who became famous throughout the world as the prima ballerina of the Imperial Ballet Company.

Exercise 10B, 3a   "The Dead" concludes the collection of short stories, *Dubliners*, in which Irish author James Joyce (1882–1941) offers critical sketches of Dublin life.

Exercise 10B, 3c   Indefatigable in his medical studies, experiments, and writing, French physician Dr. René Laennec (1781–1826) gained world renown for advances in clinical analysis and diagnosis.

Exercise 10B, 5a   In Greek mythology Medea aids Jason in the Argonauts' search for the Golden Fleece and bears him two children.

Exercise 10B, 5b   Recipient of the 1988 Nobel Prize for Literature, Naguib Mahfouz (b. 1911) has made short stories and novels popular in Egypt, using realistic scenes from city life.

Exercise 10B, 6b   One of the only two women represented in Impressionist exhibitions in Paris, French artist Berthe Morisot (1841–1895) earned early support from recognized painters and later had great influence on the work of Édouard Manet.

Exercise 10C, 3   In *The Rivals*, Richard Brinsley Sheridan (1751–1816) satirizes affectations and excesses of people gathered at Bath to enjoy the English social season and the spa.

Exercise 10C, 4	Awarded the Pulitzer Prize for Literature in 1987, *Beloved* followed other fiction by African-American novelist Toni Morrison (b. 1931).
Exercise 10C, 5	With *Volpone* in 1606, English poet and playwright Ben Jonson (1573?–1637) captures the farcical struggles of bourgeois characters to get rich at the death of a relative.
Exercise 10C, 10	The author of more than 500 books, Isaac Asimov (1920–1992) attributed his capacity to learn and transmit information in many genres to his being the "beneficiary of a lucky break in the genetic sweepstakes."
Exercise 10C, 11	After convincing the hesitant Dauphin of France that her saintly voices assured success, Joan of Arc (1412?–1431) led the troops to victory over English forces. She was later imprisoned and burned at the stake for heresy.
Exercise 10D	As the first woman in space, Russian astronaut Valentina Tereshkova-Nikolayeva (b. 1937) spent 70 hours and 50 minutes completing 48 orbits and traveling 1.2 million miles.

NOTA BENE: Both Latin and Greek distinguish between "upper air" *(ether)* and "lower air," *aer,* from which come *aerial, Ariel, aerobatics, aerobic, aerodynamics, aeronaut,* and *aerospace.*

INTRODUCE Lesson 10

(Book D, page 86)

Remind students that the theme of Lessons 10 and 11 is "Earth and Air."

Display, read, and translate this Latin expression (from page 86 of Lesson 10): *In aere picardi; in mare venaris.* "To fish in the air; to hunt in the sea."

- Have students use their own words to describe what it means to fish in the air and hunt in the sea. (Sample: to look for something where it normally doesn't exist; to dream, often unrealistically)
- Tell students that Latin and Greek roots having to do with air appear in some of the words to learn in Lesson 10.

PREVIEW Familiar Words

(Book D, pages 86-89)

animation, phantom, fantasy, inspire, perspire, hypersensitive, ventilate

ACTIVITY 1

The Latin *anima* ("wind," "air") and *animus* ("mind," "soul") are sources of English words with the root *anim*. Help students understand that other meanings have grown from the root.

Display the familiar word *animation.*

Read aloud each sentence below, and discuss what *animation* means in each one:

- The cartoon's medium was computer *animation.* (seeming action, as in a movie)
- Gina's face shows *animation* when she talks. (movement, expressiveness)

Tell students that the word *animation* names things that are or appear to be full of life.

The original Latin root, *animus,* named the soul, or the life source.

ACTIVITY 2

The Greek *phanein* ("to show," "to appear") is the source of English words with the root *phan/fan*. Help students make meaning connections.

Display the familiar words *phantom* and *fantasy.*

Tell students that the roots *phan/fan* come from a Greek word meaning "to appear."

Ask: What might the meaning connection be between the Greek root and the English words? (Samples: A *phantom* is something that does not exist but *appears* to be real./A *fantasy* is imagery that *appears* in someone's imagination.)

ACTIVITY 3

The Latin *spirare* ("to blow gently," "to breathe") and related forms are sources of English words with the root *spir(e)*. Help students understand that other meanings have grown from the root.

Display the familiar words *inspire* and *perspire.*

Have students name the root that appears in both words. *(spire)*

Tell students that a Latin word meaning "to blow gently" or "to breathe" is the source of the root *spire* in both words. Discuss what each word might have to do with breathing. (Sample: *Perspiring* is a way for your skin to *breathe.*/To *inspire* is to *breathe* new meaning into something.)

ACTIVITY 4

The Greek *huper* ("over," "above") is the source of the English-language prefix *hyper*. Help students think about the root meaning.

Display the familiar word *hypersensitive*.

Have students demonstrate a *hypersensitive* response to the statement, "Please remember to put your name at the top of your paper."

Tell students that the prefix *hyper* adds the meaning "super" or "over" to words.

ACTIVITY 5

The Latin *ventus* ("wind") is a source of English words with the root *vent*. Help students think about the root meaning.

Display the familiar word *ventilate*.

Ask students to demonstrate what they would do to *ventilate* a room. (Sample: open a window; turn on a fan)

Point out the root *vent*, explaining that it comes from a Latin word meaning "wind."

ACTIVITY 6: Antonym Prefixes

Have students distinguish between the definitions and pronunciations of the words *hypercritical* and *hypocritical* (from Lesson 3). (Sample: The prefix "hyper" means "over" and "hypo" is its opposite. To be *hypercritical* is to be overly critical, and *hypocritical* behavior implies sneakiness or underhanded judgment of other people.)

ACTIVITY 7: Review Familiar Words

Review by having students identify the root in each displayed word. Lesson 10 also includes the Latin *aether* ("upper air," "clear sky") and Greek *aither* ("air"), sources of English words with the root *ether*.

PRESENT Key Words

(Book D, pages 86–89)

Direct students to read the six roots and root families boldfaced on pages 86–89 of their Level D books. Then have them turn to page 86 to read the boxed key words chorally: *animus, aspiration, diaphanous, dispirited, epiphany, equanimity, ether, ethereal, hyperbole, hyperborean, hyperventilation, phantasm, pusillanimous, sycophant, vent.*

Present each key word by discussing the following:

- pronunciation
- definitions/connections to the root
- sentences
- parts of speech
- word forms

Use the *Nota Bene* after *hyperborean* to play a dictionary game with the prefix *hyper-*. Give students thirty seconds to copy as many words from the dictionary with this prefix as they can, then shut their books and try to explain the definitions.

Use the *Nota Bene* after *vent* to have students explain why *deflated* and *dispirited* are synonyms. (Sample: both mean "dejected," as in the metaphorical and physical loss of air associated with a sigh.)

GUIDE Practice

Key Words Q&A

- What is a treatment for *hyperventilation*? (Sample: breathing into a paper bag)

- Would you like to vacation in a *hyperborean* region? Why or why not? (Samples: Yes, I would enjoy the beautiful scenery./No, it would be too cold.)

- What advice would you give to a *dispirited* friend? (Sample: Cheer up! Tomorrow is a new day.)

- Do you have professional *aspirations*? If yes, what are they? (Samples: Yes, to be a doctor/lawyer/teacher/athlete./Not yet, I want to pursue a variety of interests.)

- What is an appropriate way to *vent* one's anger? (Samples: Talk to the person you're angry with./Do some exercise./Write in a journal.)

- Could a scientist have an *epiphany*? Why do you think that? (Sample: Yes, a scientist could suddenly realize a new way to perform an experiment or experience a breakthrough.)

- What causes some people to lose their *equanimity*? (Sample: being asked a question they don't know the answer to/getting caught driving in a rainstorm)

- Why was the discovery of *ether* such a medical breakthrough? (Sample: It was used as an anesthetic, to numb the pain of surgery.)

- Why does ruthlessness often lead to *animus*? (Sample: When people are ruthless they are cruel and without pity, leading to feelings of animosity by those they encounter.)

- What do *diaphanous* drapes look like? (Sample: They are translucent, flowing.)
- Is it a compliment to call someone *sycophantic*? Why or why not? (Sample: No, it's like calling someone a kiss-up.)
- Do you believe that sportscasters make *hyperbolic* comments about athletes and teams? Why do you say that? (Sample: Yes, sportscasters use hyperbolic language—the best in the world, the most important match of her career—to engage fans' interest and heighten their excitement of an athlete or team.)
- In what way is a mirage a *phantasm*? (Sample: A mirage appears real, but is merely an apparition.)
- If a critic describes a ballet performance as *ethereal*, is the review favorable? Why do you say that? (Sample: Yes, it means the dancers are light on their feet.)
- What animals are usually thought of as *pusillanimous*? (Sample: the Cowardly Lion, elephants when they see a mouse)

Lesson 10 Key Word Activity Master (see page 124)

Answers:

1. an epiphany
2. a dispirited condition
3. hyperventilation
4. diaphanous fabric
5. the animus to heroism
6. equanimity
7. a phantasm
8. the ether
9. hyperbole
10. hyperborean aspiration
11. venting one's animus
12. a pusillanimous sycophant
13. ethereal aspirations

ASSIGN Exercises

Book D, pages 90–94

REVIEW Lessons 9 and 10

Guide students in a game of Team Definitions.

- Display the challenge words for Lessons 9 and 10.

- Divide the group into two teams.

- Have a member of Team A secretly choose one of the words and read aloud its first definition in the dictionary. (If the word itself appears in the definition, the reader should substitute the word *blank*.)

- Members of Team B work together to name the word with just one guess. If they name it, they earn three points. If they do not name it, the other members of Team A have a chance to guess the word and earn three points.

- The dictionary reader continues with any additional definitions until the word is guessed. (Guessing on the second try earns two points; subsequent guesses earn one point.)

SELECT Review Exercises

Book D, pages 94–96

LESSON 11

Literary and Historical References

4. flagrant
Founded in 1961 and awarded the Nobel Peace Prize in 1977, Amnesty International is "an independent movement working impartially for the release of all prisoners of conscience, fair and prompt trials for political prisoners, and an end to torture and executions."

5. inflammatory
Alice Hamilton (1869–1970), an American physician, toxicologist, and teacher, became an authority on poisons and related ailments especially as they applied to industrial conditions.

6. flamboyant
An observance going back to the fourth century, the penitential period of Lent is usually preceded by a time of celebration known as Mardi Gras or carnival.

7. incendiary
Slaughterhouse Five by American author Kurt Vonnegut (b. 1922) presents an account of the futility of war, desecration of a beautiful old city, and the surreal aftermath for some of the survivors.

South African politician and outspoken foe of apartheid, Helen Suzman (b. 1917) has received numerous human rights awards.

8. incense
In "The Rape of the Lock" English poet Alexander Pope (1688–1744) satirizes the fury of the victim Belinda at the loss of a lock of hair.

9. caustic
Alice Roosevelt Longworth (1884–1980), the spirited daughter of President Theodore Roosevelt, enjoyed social life and was often sharptongued, as when she resisted a kiss from her cousin, President Franklin D. Roosevelt.

12. pyrotechnics
African-American musician Bobby McFerrin (b. 1950) is a singer, instrumentalist, and conductor of symphony orchestras.

15. scintillate
An American actress in film and stage musicals, Mary Martin (1913–1990) dominated musical comedy for decades.

Exercise 11B, 1b
Permitted to return to Spain in 1977 after the death of dictator Francisco Franco, Dolores Ibarruri (1895–1989), an ardent Communist and political activist, was returned to Parliament at age 81.

Exercise 11B, 2c Denied a concert site, African-American contralto Marian Anderson (1902–1993) later performed at the Lincoln Memorial in Washington, D.C., before a crowd of 75,000; she became in 1955 the first black member of the Metropolitan Opera Company.

Exercise 11B, 3b The foremost naval authority of his time, English diarist Samuel Pepys (1633–1703) is best remembered today for his personal record of the 1660s that includes the plague (1665) and the great fire (1666).

Exercise 11B, 4b American author William Faulkner (1897–1962) depicts strained relationships in the Snopes family in this story and other fictional works.

Exercise 11B, 4d Few people from the past are quoted as often as Samuel Johnson (1709–1784), whose epigrams were collected by his biographer James Boswell (1740–1795) for *The Life of Samuel Johnson* (1791).

Exercise 11B, 5a Historians now believe the alleged love affair between Ann Rutledge and Abraham Lincoln to have been contrived by William Herndon (1818– 1891), Lincoln's law partner and biographer, as an expression of dislike for Mary Lincoln.

Exercise 11B, 6d In *The Divine Comedy* by Dante Alighieri (1265–1321), the Italian poet journeys through the Inferno and Purgatory to Paradise; the incendiary rain falls in Canto 15 of the Inferno.

Exercise 11B, 7a American journalist Tom Wolfe (b. 1931) is also the author of *The Right Stuff* (1979) and *The Bonfire of the Vanities* (1987).

Exercise 11B, 7b African-American soprano Kathleen Battle (b. 1948) dazzles opera-goers around the world in Mozart operas, among them *The Magic Flute, Don Giovanni,* and *Abduction from the Seraglio.*

Exercise 11C, 4 Known for her short stories, poems, and plays, Dorothy Parker (1893– 1967) was one of the founders of the Round Table of writers and artists who met regularly at the Algonquin Hotel in New York City.

NOTA BENE: Students may be interested in other "warm" words and their derivatives. The Latin word for "fire" is *ignis*, which gives to English *ignite, ignition, igneous, ignescent,* and *ignis fatuus,* the last of which means "foolish fire," "will-o'-the-wisp," or "swamp fire." The Latin verb *caleo, calere, calui, calidum* means "to be warm"; from it come the English words *camouflage, caldron, chafe, nonchalant,* and *scald.* From the Latin word *sol* are derived *solar, parasol, solarium,* and *solstice.*

INTRODUCE Lesson 11

(Book D, page 97)

Tell students that the theme of Lessons 11 and 12 is "Fire and Water."

Display, read, and translate this Latin quotation (from page 97 of Lesson 11): *Parva saepe scintilla contempta excitavit incendium.* "Often a small ignored spark has started a fire."

- Ask students for their ideas about the meaning of the quotation. Note that English-speakers have a similar proverb: "Of a small spark, a great fire." Another proverb with the same message is "A small leak will sink a great ship." (Sample: Something that seems small might have large consequences.)
- Point out *scintilla* and *incendium*, telling students that English words with Latin roots for "spark" and "fire" are among the words to learn in Lesson 11.

PREVIEW Familiar Words

(Book D, pages 98–101)

flame, flamingo, calm, tinsel

ACTIVITY 1

The Latin *flamma* ("flame") is the source of English words with the root *flam.* Help students make meaning connections.

Display the familiar words *flame* and *flamingo.*

Point out the root *flam*, explaining that it comes from a Latin word meaning "flame."

Ask: What do you think is the meaning connection between *flame* and *flamingo*? (Sample: A *flamingo's* color is as bright as a *flame.*)

ACTIVITY 2

The Greek *kaiein* ("to burn") is the source of English words with the root *cau(s)t.* Help students understand that other meanings have grown from the root.

Display the familiar word *calm* and tell students it comes from the Greek root *kaiein* meaning "to burn."

Point out that the displayed word *calm* seems to have nothing to do with the root meaning "to burn," and ask students if they can think of any connection between the two. Ask a student to read aloud the dictionary derivation of *calm.* (The Greek *kauma*, "burning heat," was used by Latin speakers as *cauma* to name a spot to rest during the hottest part of the day.)

ACTIVITY 3

The Latin *scintilla* ("spark") is the source of English words with the root *scintilla*. Help students think about the root meaning.

Display the familiar word *tinsel*.

Ask students to describe *tinsel*. (Sample: It is a kind of decoration that glitters and *sparkles*.)

Tell students that the word *tinsel* retains the root meaning of "spark," from the Latin *scintilla*. The consonant sounds /s/ and /t/ were reversed, however, as the word passed from Latin into English.

ACTIVITY 4: Review Familiar Words

Review by having students name a displayed word with the Latin root *flamma* ("flame," "flamingo"); the Greek root *kaiein* ("calm"); and the Latin root *scintilla* ("tinsel"). Lesson 11 also includes the Latin *fervere* ("to be boiling hot"); *flagrare* ("to glow," "to burn," "to blaze"); *incendere* ("to set on fire"); and the Greek *pur* ("fire").

PRESENT Key Words

(Book D, pages 97–101)

Direct students to read the seven roots and root families boldfaced on pages 97–101 of their Level D books. Then have them turn to page 97 to read the boxed key words chorally: *caustic, cauterize, conflagration, effervescent, fervid, flagrant, flamboyant, incendiary, incense, inflammatory, pyre, pyromania, pyrotechnics, scintilla, scintillate.*

Present each key word by discussing the following:

- pronunciation
- definitions/connections to the root
- sentences
- parts of speech
- word forms

Use the *Nota Bene* after *flamboyant* to point out that *flammable* and *inflammable* are synonyms. Explain that because the prefix *in-* can mean "not," people sometimes mistakenly think that an inflammable material won't burn, when the opposite is true. Tell students to remember that the prefix *in-* in *inflammable* is like *en-*, and adds the meaning "in" or "completely" to the word that follows.

Use the *Nota Bene* with *incense* to explain that the aromatic substance *incense* and the action to *incense* come from the same Latin root meaning "to set on fire." Because the words took different paths from that original root, however, the words are considered homographs and usually have separate entries in a dictionary.

Use the *Nota Bene* after *scintillate* to discuss the additional Latin root *sol*. Have students brainstorm compound terms in which the first word is *solar*. (Samples: solar wind, solar panel, solar system, solar battery)

GUIDE Practice

For Example

Ask for examples of each of the following:

- things that can *scintillate* (Samples: jewels, dewdrops, sequins, conversation)
- places to see *pyrotechnics* (Samples: a Fourth of July celebration, a rock concert)
- something said in a *caustic* tone of voice (Sample: have students say the phrase "I really love it" in a sarcastic tone versus a serious tone.)
- ways people can avoid starting *conflagrations* in the woods (Samples: make sure their campfire is completely out; don't smoke)
- what people say when they are *incensed* (Samples: "How dare you!" "Now I'm really mad.")
- things that can be *inflammatory* (Samples: insulting comments; a political speech; a place on the skin where a bee has stung; a body part that has been injured)
- what people say when they are *fervid* about an issue (Samples: "I am absolutely right!" "When you learn the facts, you will join our cause." "This is the most important problem facing the world today.")
- things that can be *effervescent* (Samples: carbonated drinks, bubble baths, personalities, conversation)
- purposes of a *pyre* (Samples: to burn a body during a funeral rite; to burn any pile of flammable materials; to celebrate with a bonfire)
- purposes of *cauterizing* (Samples: to stop bleeding; to prevent infection in a wound)
- examples of celebrities who dress in a *flamboyant* styles (Answers will vary.)
- *incendiary* remarks between rival sports fans (Samples: "My team is the best!" "Your team stinks!")
- traits of a *flagrant pyromaniac* (Sample: the person sets fires openly without trying to conceal clues)
- how you can tell that someone feels a *scintilla* of fear (Sample: the person's eyes open slightly wider; he or she makes a small gasp.)

Lesson 11 Key Word Activity Master (see page 125)

Answers:

1. pyrotechnics
2. incense
3. flagrant
4. cauterize
5. scintilla
6. effervescent
7. incendiary
8. flamboyant
9. caustic
10. scintillate
11. pyre
12. inflammatory
13. conflagration
14. pyromania
15. fervid

ASSIGN Exercises

Book D, pages 101–105

LESSON 12

Literary and Historical References

3. flux
A volcanic explosion on Heimaey in 1973 covered the island with lava, but inhabitants were able to return a year later to their homes and a much improved harbor.

Countries frequently ravaged by drought and warfare in the Horn of Africa are Ethiopia, Somalia, and Sudan.

5. hydrology
Called "the Ancient Ones" and known to have lived in the Southwest from A.D. 100 to 1300, the Anasazi people understood irrigation and terracing, and as pueblo dwellers they cultivated crafts of basket making and pottery much admired in the twentieth century.

10. pontiff
During the process of electing a new pontiff, a stove in the Sistine Chapel where ballots are cast and then burned has a special mechanism to produce black smoke (straw mixed with paper) for no decision or white smoke for a successful election; the smoke informs crowds waiting for the news.

11. pontificate
Lasting from 1378 to 1417, the Great Schism between Avignon and Rome arose when the cardinals refused to accept the election of arrogant Pope Urban VI and ended with the election of a new pope, Martin V.

12. undulate
English poet Percy Bysshe Shelley (1792–1822) addresses 324 lines, including mention of "undulating corn," to a valued friend in the poem "Letter to Maria Gisbourne."

13. redound
Recipient of the 1983 Nobel Prize for Medicine or Physiology, American geneticist Barbara McClintock waited many years for other scientists to accept her 1951 analysis of generations of maize that showed genes not fixed in place but able to jump around on a chromosome.

15. inundate
According to Genesis 9:9-17, God promises Noah that the earth will never again be inundated (Genesis 6-9).

Exercise 12B, 3c
Because she was divorced and the mother of two children, socialite Emily Price Post (1872–1960) had to earn a living as a society reporter until she wrote *Etiquette* (1922), which gave readers detailed advice for handling social situations.

Exercise 12B, 3d
Pope John XXIII (1881–1963) became a forceful spokesperson for international understanding and initiated the Second Vatican Council in 1962 for discussion of reform and unity within the world-wide Catholic church.

Exercise 12B, 5b Completed in 1970, the Aswan Dam serves both Egypt and the Sudan; however, the soil made available for cultivation is less fertile because valuable silt is deflected into reservoirs and canals.

Exercise 12B, 5c When Plato wrote about Atlantis in 300 B.C., he encouraged belief in the legend of an island sunk into the ocean, which some scholars believe to be Thira, north of Crete in the Aegean Sea, where, around 1500 B.C., inundation after a volcanic explosion destroyed half of the island.

Exercise 12B, 6b Starting with a tiny instrument on her third birthday and playing Bartok and Paganini at age ten, Japanese prodigy Midori (b. 1971) is now a professional violinist.

Exercise 12B, 6c Beautiful and enigmatic, Swedish film actress Greta Garbo, born Greta Lovisa Gustafsson (1905–1990), remains much admired for her roles in *Anna Christie, Camille,* and *Ninotchka.*

Exercise 12B, 9c Ironic treatment of current and personal events appears in the newspaper columns and memoirs of American journalist Russell Baker (b. 1925).

Exercise 12B, 9d American chef Julia Child (1912–2004) turned her expertise into cookbooks and television programs, featuring principles of French cuisine adapted to American kitchens and palates.

Exercise 12C, 1 Fastidious in style and relentless in maintaining integrity, American journalist Harry Reasoner (1923–1991) was most recently a member of the Columbia Broadcasting System news staff.

Exercise 12D The basilica of Hagia Sophia in Istanbul, Turkey, completed in 537 under Emperor Justinian, was the heart of the Eastern Orthodox Christian Church. When the city of Constantinople fell to the Turks in 1453, the Hagia Sophia became a mosque for Muslim worshippers. Mustafa Kemal Ataturk turned it into a museum during his presidency (1923–1938).

INTRODUCE Lesson 12

(Book D, page 105)

Remind students that the theme of Lessons 11 and 12 is "Fire and Water."

Display, read, and translate this Latin expression (from page 105 of Lesson 12): *Amicus magis necessarium quam ignis aut aqua.* "A friend is more necessary than fire or water."

- Ask students to identify any of the Latin words they can match to English ones. Students may recognize *aqua*, Latin for "water," in words such as *aquamarine, aquarium,* and *aquatic.* They might also recognize *ignis*, Latin for "fire," the root of which appears in English words *ignite* and *ignition.* *Necessarium* can also be paired with "necessary," and *amicus* with "amicable" or friendly.

- Ask students why it might be just as important to have a friend as to have basic necessities such as fire or water.

- Tell students that other Latin and Greek roots having to do with water are in English words to learn in Lesson 12.

PREVIEW Familiar Words

(Book D, pages 106–109)

affluent, fluent, fluid, hydrogen, marina, marine, mariner, abundance

ACTIVITY 1

The Latin *fluere* ("to flow") and related forms are sources of English words with the root *flu(x)*. Help students compare and contrast words with the root.

Display the familiar words *affluent, fluent,* and *fluid.*

Read aloud each sentence below with the emphasis shown. Direct students to end the sentence with one of the displayed words:

- A second language seems to flow effortlessly from someone who has studied to be (fluent).
- Any liquid that flows is called a (fluid).
- A dancer's graceful, flowing movements are (fluid).
- Money seems to flow from the pockets of those who are (affluent).

Ask: What is a meaning of the root *flu*? ("flowing")

ACTIVITY 2

The Greek *hudor* ("water") is the source of English words with the root *hydr(o)*. Help students think about the root meaning.

Display the familiar word *hydrogen*.

Point out the root *hydr*, telling students that it comes from a Greek word for "water."

Ask: Think about your science classes to describe how the root meaning is apparent in the word *hydrogen*. (Samples: *Water* is generated by the combustion of *hydrogen*. *Water* is made up of two parts *hydrogen* to one part oxygen (H20).

ACTIVITY 3

The Latin *maris* ("sea") and related forms are sources of English words with the root *mar*. Help students think about the root meaning.

Display the familiar word *marina, marine,* and *mariner*.

Point to the root *mar*, telling students that it comes from a Latin word for "sea."

Ask: Where are the differences and similarities in pronunciation and definitions of these three words? (Sample: a *marina* is where boats can dock in the *sea; marine* means "of or relating to the *sea*"; a *marine* is someone trained militarily to fight on land or *sea*; a *mariner* is a person who navigates the *sea*.

Have students use three of the displayed words in a sentence. (Sample: The *mariner* and the *marine* shared stories of the sea on the dock of the *marina*.)

ACTIVITY 4

The Latin *unda* ("wave of the sea") is the source of English words with the root *und*. Help students make meaning connections.

Display the familiar word *abundance*.

Have students tell what an *abundance* is, and name things that can be *abundant*. (Samples: an *abundance* is an ample quantity or surplus. Thing that can be a*bundant* include food at a banquet, water in the sea, and snow in Alaska.)

Point to the root *und*, telling students that it comes from a Latin word that means "sea wave."

Ask: What meaning connection might there be between a *wave* and *abundance*? (Sample: Waves flow as if there is an endless supply. Things that are *abundant* are overflowing like *waves*.)

ACTIVITY 5: Review Familiar Words

Review by having students name a displayed word with a root that means "wave" ("abundance"); "water" ("hydrogen"); "sea" ("marina," "marine," "mariner"); and "flow" ("affluent," "fluent," "fluid"). Lesson 12 also includes the Greek *naus* ("ship") and *nautes* ("sailor") and the Latin *navis* ("ship") and *nauta* ("sailor"), sources of English words with the roots *naus/naut* and *nav*; in addition to the Latin *pontis* ("bridge"), source of English words with the root *pont*.

PRESENT Key Words

(Book D, pages 105–109)

Direct students to read the roots and root families boldfaced on pages 106–109 of their Level D books. Then have them turn to page 105 to read the boxed key words chorally: *confluence, cormorant, dehydrate, effluent, flux, hydrology, inundate, marinade, nauseate, nave, pontiff, pontificate, redound, redundant, undulate.*

Present each key word by discussing the following:

- pronunciation
- definitions/connections to the root
- sentences
- parts of speech
- word forms

Use the *Nota Bene* for *nauseate* to point out that the distinction between *nauseous* and *nauseated* is disappearing, though careful writers and speakers still avoid describing themselves as nauseous.

GUIDE Practice

Paraphrase Phrases

Have students use their own words to tell what each of these expressions means, then make up examples to illustrate their definitions:

- a spicy *marinade* (Sample: a liquid with flavorful seasonings used before cooking. Examples: barbeque sauce, spicy peanut dressing, hot sauce)

- a *nauseating* sight (Sample: a sight that makes you sick to your stomach. Examples: other people getting sick; violence on television)

- a *confluence* of fortunate events (Sample: the coming together of lucky happenings. Example: studying all the right things and getting a perfect score on a test)

- the *hydrologist's* report to the building committee (Sample: the data gathered by the scientist studying the flow of water at a planned building site. Example: the site shows possible flood damage)

- in a state of *flux* (Sample: undergoing changing conditions. Examples: being a teenager; moving with your family to a new city; your emotions while waiting for college acceptance letters)

- a thoughtless remark that *redounded* (Sample: a comment that later caused problems for the speaker. Example: "I always do better on math tests than you do.")

- where one might find *cormorants* diving for fish (Sample: marine birds fishing underwater. Examples: the sea, a beach, the ocean)

- things located at the *nave* of the church (Sample: the central section of the building between the altar and entrance. Examples: pews, bookshelves, collection basket)

- state a viewpoint without *pontificating* (Sample: express an opinion without sounding like a know-it-all. Example: "I really think the answer is B, but let's do some research together to double-check.")

- why someone might suffer from *dehydration* (Sample: become physically ill due to lack of water. Examples: exercising without drinking enough water; taking a long ride in a non-air conditioned car with the windows up)

- the *effluent* from factories into the river (Sample: the waste materials that flow into the river. Example: chemicals used in a factory)

- *inundated* with assignments (Sample: flooded with things to do; overwhelmed. Examples: too much homework; lots of chores at home)

- the gently *undulating* landscape (Sample: the land has small, regular rises and drops. Examples: hills, a small mountain chain)

- the authority of the *pontiff* (Sample: the power of the pope. Example: religious dictates by a pope)

- *redundant* words (Sample: words that are unnecessary because they repeat an already given meaning. Examples: very unique; best ever; exact same)

Lesson 12 Key Word Activity Master (see page 126)

Answers:

1. undulations
2. marinade
3. cormorants
4. nauseated
5. pontiff
6. redound
7. redundancy

8. hydrology

9. confluence

10. dehydration

11. effluent

12. inundated

13. flux

14. pontificate

15. nave

ASSIGN Exercises

Book D, pages 109–113

REVIEW Lessons 11 and 12

Ask one student to read aloud each of the thirty key words while listeners take turns explaining its meaning connection to the root. For example: *Things that are redundant are like an overflow from a "wave."/Pyrotechnics are "fireworks."* For words in which the meaning connection is not apparent—*pontificate*, for example—have a student use a dictionary to read aloud the derivation.

SELECT Review Exercises

Book D, pages 113–116

LESSON 13

Literary and Historical References

1. insubordinate   In the novel *Oliver Twist*, Charles Dickens (1812–1870) depicts the harsh treatment pupils received in institutions run by malevolent profiteers.

2. inordinate   Receiving gifts from every god (her name means "gift of all"), Pandora is a beautiful but duplicitous creature dispersing troubles among humankind, but in the more familiar version of the myth she is just excessively curious, managing to shut the box before hope escapes.

3. ordain   Recipient of the 1964 Nobel Peace Prize, Martin Luther King, Jr., (1929–1968) is remembered for successful nonviolent boycotts, voter registration drives, and the peaceful march on Washington that drew a crowd of thousands.

4. ordinance   Ramadan, celebrated in the ninth month of the Muslim year, requires that believers fast and forgo all forms of indulgence.

5. apostle   American zoologist Rachel Carson (1907–1964), who wrote engagingly about science, also warned against indiscriminate use of insecticides.

6. stolid   Ardent in the cause of women's rights, Elizabeth Cady Stanton (1815–1902) worked with Susan B. Anthony (1820–1906) for suffrage and also for temperance laws and abolition of slavery.

7. epistolary   Many extended absences of her husband John Adams and other family members gave Abigail Adams (1744–1818) frequent opportunity to express herself through warm, lively, and informative letters.

8. rectify   Ada Deer (b. 1935) of the Menominee nation has been active in political and social issues and is a leader of a Native American women's network, OHOYO, meaning "woman" in the Choctaw language.

10. constellation   Two of the notable members of The Club were Dr. Samuel Johnson (1709–1784), compiler of *The Dictionary of the English Language* (1755), and English actor and theater manager David Garrick (1717–1779), whose innovations in acting style and theater lighting and staging are in use today.

11. stellar

In the bull ring Conchita Cintrón (b. 1922) performed on horseback and on foot as a torera, gaining highest acclaim in South America.

13. astral

Working before the invention of the telescope, Danish astronomer Tycho Brahe (1546–1601) recorded his sightings with such accuracy that later astronomers were able to use his information.

15. cosmopolite

Although successful as a commercial photographer, Lee Miller (1907– 1978) has only recently received appropriate recognition for her later photography.

Exercise 13A, 1

Concealing the fact that he has fathered Hester Prynne's child, the Reverend Mr. Arthur Dimmesdale is plagued by conscience but lets Hester alone suffer ostracism in *The Scarlet Letter* by Nathaniel Hawthorne (1804–1864).

Exercise 13B, 2c

The offspring of Soong Charles Jones had influence in China and beyond: Soong Ai-ling (1890–1973), wife of a banker and businessman; Soong Ch'ing-ling (1892–1981), wife of the Chinese Republic's first leader, Sun Yat-sen; Soong Mei-ling (b. 1898?), wife of General Chiang Kai-shek; and T. V. Soong (1894–1971), financier and government minister.

Exercise 13B, 3b

The apostle Paul (A.D. 5?–69?), writing epistles to Christians he visited as a missionary, taught salvation by faith alone, a message that fortified Martin Luther (1483–1546) in his opposition to the sale of indulgences by the Catholic church.

Exercise 13B, 3c

In the first chapter of *A Fairly Good Time*, Canadian author Mavis Gallant (b. 1922) adds this to the speaker's advice: "Undefined misery is no use to anyone."

Exercise 13B, 3d

American consumer advocate Ralph Nader (b. 1934) has exposed irregularities and injustices in such areas as automobile manufacture, pensions, atomic energy, insurance, and disability rights.

Exercise 13B, 4a

Gabriela Mistral (1889–1957) became the first Latin American to win the Nobel Prize for Literature.

Exercise 13B, 4d

Babylon rose to the status of a legend under Nebuchadnezzar in the sixth century B.C. for its temples, palaces, and hanging gardens, one of the Seven Wonders of the World.

Exercise 13B, 5c The discovery that the universe has star systems beyond the Milky Way has given American astronomer Edwin P. Hubble (1889–1953) a permanent place in history. The Hubble Space Telescope launched in 1990 bears his name.

Exercise 13B, 6a English novelist Samuel Richardson (1689–1761) introduced the epistolary novel as a form of English fiction.

Exercise 13B, 6b Norwegian dramatist Henrik Ibsen (1828–1906) wrote often about the individual's moral responsibility in political and social issues.

Exercise 13B, 7a The cows mentioned by English author Stella Gibbons (1902–1989) appear in a short story from *Conference at Cold Comfort Farm* (1949). Her humorous novel *Cold Comfort Farm* appeared in 1932.

Exercise 13B, 7b Demanding that citizens conform to Communist ideology, Soviet Communist leader Joseph Stalin (1879–1953), head of the USSR from 1924 to 1953, exiled, imprisoned, or executed dissidents.

Exercise 13B, 7d In *Heart of Darkness* Polish-born author Joseph Conrad (Teodor Józef Konrad Korzeniowski, 1857–1924) depicts depredation of Africa by European colonizers.

Exercise 13B, 8a Growing up with spirituals and now famous as an opera star, African-American soprano Jessye Norman (b. 1945) has performed in Europe, South America, Australia, and Israel.

Exercise 13B, 8b English novelist Baroness Orczy (Mrs. Montague Barstow, 1865–1947) created in *The Scarlet Pimpernel* a master of disguise who avoids detection by both friends and enemies as he performs heroic deeds.

Exercise 13B, 8c From the evidence of his student Plato, Athenian philosopher Socrates (470?–399 B.C.) advised his students, "Know thyself," encouraging them to identify with principles, not specific persons or places.

Exercise 13C, 2 The author of *The Iliad* and *The Odyssey*, Homer (9th century B.C.) introduced vivid individual characterizations.

Exercise 13C, 3 The work of Marie-Thérèse Basse (b. 1930), Director of the Institute of Food Technology in Dakar, Senegal, in developing millet bread *(pain de mil)* has significantly alleviated food shortages in countries bordering the Sahara.

Exercise 13C, 4 English author Fay Weldon (b. 1933) writes about women's issues and family relationships in her novels, plays, and television dramas.

Exercise 13C, 8   Winner of many scientific medals and honors, American astronomer Allan Rex Sandage (b. 1926) is Professor of Physics at Johns Hopkins University and Senior Research Astronomer at the Space Telescope Scientific Institute.

Exercise 13C, 10   According to the testimony of Dr. Samuel Mudd (1833–1883), he had not heard that President Lincoln had been assassinated until after the departure of the injured John Wilkes Booth (1838–1865), who was discovered and shot two weeks later.

INTRODUCE Lesson 13

(Book D, page 117)

Tell students that the theme of Lessons 13 and 14 is "Order and Disorder in the Universe."

Display, read, and translate this Latin quotation (from page 117 of Lesson 13): *Non est ad astra mollis a terris via.* "The way from the earth to the stars is not easy."

- Tell students that the quotation comes from a work by Seneca, an ancient Roman philosopher who served as tutor to the emperor Nero.
- Ask students to identify any of the Latin words they can match to English ones. They should recognize *terris*, "earth," from Lesson 9. They may also recognize *astra*, "stars."
- Tell students that a Latin proverb expressing the same idea is the state motto of Kansas: *Ad astra per aspera* ("To the stars through difficulties.")
- Ask students if they can think of expressions in English that have a similar meaning or use the symbol of catching stars (Samples: "Reach for the stars." "Catch a falling star.")
- Tell students that English words with the root *aster*, meaning "star," are among the words to learn in Lesson 13.

PREVIEW Familiar Words

(Book D, pages 117–120)

disorder, subordinate, rectangle, disaster, macrocosm, microcosm

ACTIVITY 1

The Latin *ordo* ("order," "series," "row," "line") and related forms are sources of English words with the root *ord*. Help students think about word parts and root meanings.

Display the familiar words *disorder* and *subordinate.*

Ask: Which word literally means "opposite of order"? (disorder)

Ask: Which word literally means "to put lower in the order"? (subordinate)

What is a meaning for the Latin root *ord*? (order)

ACTIVITY 2

The Latin *regere* ("to guide," "to govern") and related forms are sources of English words with the root *rect/reg*. Help students make meaning connections.

Display the familiar word *rectangle.*

Tell students that the root *rect* comes from a Latin word having to do with guiding or ruling.

Have students draw a rectangle. Ask: What meaning connection might there be between *rectangle* and the Latin root? (Sample: The shape of a rectangle is *governed* by mathematical rules [i.e. a rectangle always has four sides, forming right angles]; when drawing a rectangle, your pencil is *guided* to create four straight lines and right angles.)

ACTIVITY 3

The Greek and Latin *aster* ("star") is the source of English words with the root *ast(e)r*. Help students understand that other meanings have grown from the root.

Display the familiar word *disaster.*

Ask students for examples of natural disasters. (Samples: hurricane, tornado, volcanic eruption)

Explain that the literal translation of *disaster* has an obsolete definition, one no longer used by English speakers: "a bad influence from the stars."

Discuss the way in which the meaning of *disaster* changed from its original connection to the root *aster*, "star." Students may know that before the science of astronomy existed, astrology was influential. People believed that the position of heavenly bodies affected human events. When the stars were in an unfavorable position, a bad event resulted—a "dis-aster."

ACTIVITY 4

The Greek *kosmos* ("universe") is the source of English words with the root *cosm(o)*. Help students understand that other meanings have grown from the root.

Display the familiar words *macrocosm* and *microcosm*.

Ask: Using the prefixes and roots, tell the difference between these words. (Sample: a *microcosm* is a tiny sampling of the whole universe; a *macrocosm* includes the whole universe)

Have a student read the dictionary definitions and use both words in sentences that demonstrate meaning. Discuss usage of these terms (often metaphorical or descriptive).

ACTIVITY 5: Nouns and Verbs

Ask students to write a sentence with *subordinate* as a noun, and a sentence with it as a verb. Have them read aloud their sentences to hear the shift in syllable stress. Discuss differences in shades of meaning. (Samples: The office assistant is the boss's *subordinate* [noun]; Do not *subordinate* yourself to the whims of a domineering friend [verb]).

ACTIVITY 6: Review Familiar Words

Review by having students give a meaning for the Lesson 13 roots *ord* ("order," "series," "row," "line"); *rect* ("guide," "govern"); *aster* ("star"); and *cosmo* ("universe"). Lesson 13 also includes the Greek *stellein* ("to put," "to place"), source of English words with the root *stol*; and the Latin *stella* ("star"), source of English words with the root *stella*.

PRESENT Key Words

(Book D, pages 117–121)

Direct students to read the six roots and root families boldfaced on pages 117–120 of their Level D books. Then have them turn to page 117 to read the boxed key words chorally: *apostle, asterisk, astral, constellation, cosmology, cosmopolite, epistolary, inordinate, insubordinate, ordain, ordinance, rectify, rectitude, stellar, stolid.*

Present each key word by discussing the following:

- pronunciation
- definitions/connections to the root
- sentences
- parts of speech
- word forms

Use the *Nota Bene* with *astral* to point out that synonyms, such as *astral* and *stellar*, are rarely identical and interchangeable in English. Connotation and usages vary. Ask: What types of performances can be described as *stellar*? (Samples: a great concert, high marks on a test) Would you describe those performances as *astral*? Why or why not?

GUIDE Practice

Key Word Q&A

- Would you like to become a *cosmopolite*? Why or why not? (Samples: Yes, because I enjoy traveling and learning about the word./No, I am xenophobic.)

- Have you read any *epistolary* novels? (Samples: *The Color Purple, Letters from the Inside, Dear Mr. Henshaw, Dear Nobody*)

- Demonstrate *insubordinate* behavior. (Samples: raising one's voice; sticking out a tongue; ignoring the teacher)

- What *constellations* of the night sky do you recognize? (Samples: the Big Dipper, Little Dipper, Orion's Belt)

- What is an example of a local *ordinance*? (Samples: recycling, off-street parking rules, town curfew)

- Draw an *astral* shape in the air. (Sample: students should trace a star shape)

- Who in modern times could be called an *apostle* for peace? (Samples: Martin Luther King, Jr., Mother Theresa, Gandhi)

- What sciences are involved in the study of *cosmology*? (Samples: chemistry, physics, biology, astronomy)

- Which sports team can be described as *stellar*? (Samples: a baseball team that won the World Series; college basketball winners of the men's and women's NCAA tournaments; a Stanley Cup winning hockey team)

- What is a situation you wish you could *rectify*? (Samples: having studied more for a test to get a better grade; apologizing to a friend who is angry with you)

- If an *asterisk* appears in a text you are reading, what does it signal to you? (Sample: look at the bottom of the page for a footnote)

- Are you *inordinately* fond of anything? (Samples: Yes, a childhood stuffed animal I need to fall asleep./Yes, chocolate fudge ice cream I eat at least once a week./No, I have complete control over my wants and emotions.)

- Demonstrate a *stolid* response to this statement: "There will be no school tomorrow." (Sample: students should stay neutral, showing no emotion)

- Do you think it is possible to *ordain rectitude*? Why or why not? (Samples: Yes, moral codes are determined by religious beliefs./No, every individual creates his or her own belief system.)

Lesson 13 Key Word Activity Master (see page 127)

Answers:

1. constellation
2. ordinance
3. rectitude
4. rectify
5. apostles
6. stellar
7. stolidly
8. epistolary
9. asterisked
10. insubordination
11. inordinate
12. cosmopolitan
13. astral
14. ordain
15. cosmologist
16. astrophysicists

ASSIGN Exercises

Book D, pages 121–125

LESSON 14

Literary and Historical References

1. immutable
Overshadowed by four brothers, two of whom were the novelist Henry and the psychologist William, and plagued by illness much of her life, Alice James (1848–1892) began in 1889 a diary that illumines her personal struggle to define a life for herself.

4. temerity
According to Greek myth, Daedalus devises wings so that his son Icarus and he can escape from the labyrinth he himself designed.

5. temerarious
After success as an industrial photographer, Marguerite Bourke-White (1904–1971) worked for *Fortune*, documenting sharecroppers, and for *Life* magazine, as a war correspondent.

6. imperturbable
Representing one of the three generations of women whom American author Michael Dorris (b. 1945) treats in the novel *Yellow Raft on Blue Water*, Aunt Ida earns respect for equanimity and generosity won from a difficult life.

7. turbid
As a writer of literary commentary, English author Walter Savage Landor (1775–1864) was sensitive to clarity or turbidity of prose.

11. temper
The quoted line by Joseph Addison (1672–1719) appeared in the March 11, 1711, issue of *The Spectator*, a periodical produced with Richard Steele (1672–1729).

12. temperance
Known as the greatest Roman orator, Cicero (106–43 B.C.) was a master of style and delivery.

Relentless in her crusade against consumption of liquor, Carry Nation (1846–1911) believed that any property associated with saloons merited destruction, and she accepted arrest and fines as a consequence.

Exercise 14B, 1b
Writing under the pseudonym George Orwell, English author Eric Arthur Blair (1903–1950) gives bad examples in "Politics and the English Language," urging avoidance of clichés, jargon, and dead metaphors.

Exercise 14B, 2c
According to Genesis 13:10-13 and 19, God destroyed Sodom and Gomorrah because of the sinfulness of the people, sparing only Lot and his family until his wife chanced to look back.

Exercise 14B, 2d   Greek legend tells that Oedipus becomes king of Thebes, but as the inadvertent killer of his father Laertes and husband of his mother Jocasta, he is banished forever.

Exercise 14B, 3a   In her autobiography *West with the Night*, Beryl Markham (1902–1986) describes her African childhood and later adventures as an aviator, becoming the first person to fly solo across the Atlantic from east to west.

Exercise 14B, 3b   English poet laureate Alfred, Lord Tennyson (1809–1892), in the poem "The Charge of the Light Brigade" pays tribute to the bravery of the "six hundred" who rode "into the valley of Death" in the Crimea.

Exercise 14B, 3d   Other swashbuckling roles played by Errol Flynn (1909–1959) were in *The Adventures of Robin Hood* and *The Charge of the Light Brigade.*

Exercise 14B, 4a   Even as a dweller in debtor's prison, Mr. Micawber remains the comforting, sanguine father figure for David in the novel *David Copperfield* by Charles Dickens (1812–1870).

Exercise 14B, 4c   In the third part of *Gulliver's Travels*, Irish author and clergyman Jonathan Swift (1667–1745) satirizes scientific and mathematical inventions that remove scholars from reality and common sense.

Exercise 14B, 6a   In Shakespeare's play *Othello*, Iago's attempt to besmirch the good name of Desdemona is so successful that Othello is driven to strangle her before receiving proof of her innocence.

Exercise 14B, 6b   German filmmaker Leni Riefenstahl (b. 1902) was justly proud of her film of the 1936 Olympic games, but *Triumph of the Will* in 1934 made her seem a Nazi propagandist, as she notes in her *Cahiers du Cinema* (1966).

Exercise 14B, 6d   Senator from Wisconsin, Joseph McCarthy (1908–1957), gained notoriety by citing numbers of Communists who he claimed had infiltrated government, but no such infiltrators were ever uncovered.

Exercise 14B, 7b   Like other fictional immigrant women created by Willa Cather (1873–1947), Antonia embodies the tenacity and resourcefulness of American pioneers.

Exercise 14B, 8a   English novelist Laurence Sterne (1713–1768) teases readers in several ways, one of which is to let the subject of this "autobiography" in nine volumes be born in the third volume and christened in the fourth volume.

Exercise 14C, 2	According to Roman myth, the beautiful young huntress Daphne so hates love and marriage that when love-smitten Apollo runs after her, she calls to her river-god father Peneus, who turns her into a laurel tree.
Exercise 14C, 3	From 1811 to 1820 Don José Artigas aided Simón Bolívar in trying to wrest land from the wealthy and distribute it to the poor in South America; unsuccessful and called an outlaw and vagrant by the powerful, Artigas sought exile in Paraguay.
Exercise 14C, 6	The daughter of the cofounder of the Salvation Army in England, Evangeline Booth (1865–1950) served as commander of the U.S. organization and later of the International Salvation Army for 25 years.
Exercise 14C, 11	The early work of anthropologist Margaret Mead (1901–1978) dealt with primitive societies in Samoa, New Guinea, and other locations considered excessively remote for a young woman's research.
Exercise 14D	The advice given by English poet Alexander Pope (1688–1744) appears in his *Essay on Criticism* (1711).
Review Exercise 1.1	The work of Austrian author Franz Kafka (1883–1924) has supplied sharp mythic images of dissatisfaction and alienation that speak to many in the twentieth century.
Review Exercise 1.2	George Sand is the pseudonym of Amandine Aurore Lucie Dupin (1804– 1876).

INTRODUCE Lesson 14

(Book D, page 125)

Remind students that the theme of Lessons 13 and 14 is "Order and Disorder in the Universe."

Display, read, and translate this Latin expression (from page 125 of Lesson 14): *Mutatis mutandis.* "Things have been changed that had to be changed."

- Tell students that this expression appears in English writings, usually in scholarly texts. The expression may be abbreviated *m.m.* and is used when a writer wishes to make differences secondary in order to emphasize similarities. It can be paraphrased to say, "Taking differences into account, here is why two things are similar." (Sample: "My math test was as difficult as my English essay test, *mutatis mutandis.*)

- Point to the Latin word *Mutatis,* asking students whether it resembles any English words they know. Students may know *mutant, mutation,* and other words with meanings related to the Latin root "to change."

- Tell students that English words with the root *mut* are among the words to learn in Lesson 14.

PREVIEW Familiar Words

(Book D, pages 125–128)

commute, disturb, turbulence, intersperse, temperament, ultimate

ACTIVITY 1

The Latin *mutare* ("to change") and related forms are sources of English words with the root *mut*. Help students think about the root meaning.

Display the familiar word *commute*.

Tell students that the room *mut* means "change."

Ask students to provide two different definitions of the word; they may need to use a dictionary. (Samples: to travel for work; to lessen a penalty; to substitute)

Ask: What connections can you make between the word and its root meaning? (Sample: all definitions are related to change)

ACTIVITY 2

The Latin *turbare* ("to disturb," "to throw into disorder") and related forms are sources of English words with the root *turb*. Help students compare and contrast words with the root.

Display the familiar words *disturb* and *turbulence*.

Have students name the root that appears in both words *(turb)* and tell what each word has to do with the Latin root meaning "to throw into disorder." (Sample: When you throw things into *disorder*, you *disturb* them./War or political *disorder* is called a time of *turbulence*. When airplanes hit bumpy weather, they are said to be caught in *turbulence*.)

ACTIVITY 3

The Latin *spargere* ("to scatter," "to cast," "to sprinkle") and related forms are sources of English words with the root *spers(e)*. Help students think about the root meaning.

Display the familiar word *intersperse*.

Point out the root *sperse*, explaining that it comes from a Latin word meaning "to scatter."

Ask students to show handy examples of things that are *interspersed*. (Samples: *Nota Bene* paragraphs interspersed with words and definitions in their Level D books; postings interspersed with other items on the wall; any things that are distributed or "scattered" among others.)

ACTIVITY 4

The Latin *temperare* ("to combine in proportion") and related forms are sources of English words with the root *temper*. Help students make meaning connections.

Display the familiar word *temperament*.

Tell students that the root *temper* comes from a Latin word that means "to combine in proportion."

Ask: What might be combined to form a person's *temperament*? (Sample: different proportions of moodiness, lightheartedness, anger, nervousness, etc.)

ACTIVITY 5

The Latin *ultimare* ("to come to the end") and related forms are sources of English words with the root *ultim(ate)*. Help students think about the root meaning.

Display the familiar word *ultimate*.

Read aloud each phrase below, and discuss what *ultimate* means in each one:

- the *ultimate* goal (final)
- the *ultimate* sacrifice (most extreme)
- the *ultimate* gift (greatest)

Have students tell what the word *ultimate* has to do with the Latin root meaning "to come to an end." (Sample: Something *ultimate* is at the end because it is final or unsurpassed.)

ACTIVITY 6: Root Research

Tell students that during the Middle Ages, a person's *temperament* was thought to be determined by the proportions of four bodily fluids called "humors" (see Book C, page 84). The fluids and corresponding temperaments were: blood (sanguine, cheerful); phlegm (sluggish); yellow bile (choleric, easily angered); and black bile (melancholy). Each was also associated with a season and an element. Ask students to guess which humor went with which season and why. (blood—air, spring; phlegm—water, winter; yellow bile—fire, summer; black bile—earth, autumn).

ACTIVITY 7: Review Familiar Words

Review by having students identify the root and its meaning in *turbulence* (*turbare*, "to disturb," "to throw into disorder"); *ultimate* (*ultimare*, "to come to an end," "to be last"); *mutation* (*mutare*, "to change"); *intersperse* (*spargere*, "to scatter"); and *temperament* (*temperare*, "to combine in proportion"). Lesson 14 also includes the Latin *temeritas* ("rashness," "thoughtlessness").

PRESENT Key Words

(Book D, pages 125–128)

Direct students to read the six roots and root families boldfaced on pages 125–128 of their Level D books. Then have them turn to page 125 to read the boxed key words chorally: *aspersion, disperse, immutable, imperturbable, outré, penultimate, permutation, perturb, temerarious, temerity, temper, temperance, transmute, turbid, ultimatum.*

Present each key word by discussing the following:

- pronunciation
- definitions/connections to the root
- sentences
- parts of speech
- word forms

Use the *Nota Bene* with *turbid* to have students distinguish *turbid* writing ("muddy, unclear") from *turgid* writing ("swollen, bloated, ornate, grandiose"). Ask students to present an example of each, then discuss how to avoid each kind.

Use the *Nota Bene* with *temper* to have students dramatize the contrast between an "ill-tempered reaction" and a "sweet-tempered reaction."

Point out the antonyms *temperance* and *intemperance,* and have students tell what the prefix *in-* means in this case ("not," "opposite of").

GUIDE Practice

Synonyms

Have students name the key word that belongs in each list of words with similar meanings:

- recklessness, rashness, impudence,   (temerity)
- slander, slur, insinuation,   (aspersion)
- upset, agitate, disturb,   (perturb)
- invariable, unchangeable, permanent,   (immutable)
- rearrangement, transformation, transmutation,   (permutation)
- control, alleviate, show self-restraint,   (temper)
- warning, insistence, demand   (ultimatum)
- moderation, self-restraint, discipline,   (temperance)
- outrageous, eccentric, preposterous,   (outré)
- spread, scatter, disband,   (disperse)
- muddy, dark, clouded,   (turbid)

- calm, stolid, inexcitable,   (imperturbable)
- reckless, rash, bold,   (temerarious)
- transform, permute, convert,   (transmute)

Ask: What is a synonym for *next-to-last?* (penultimate) Have students use "penultimate" in a sentence. (Sample: The *penultimate* runner was relieved not to have finished last in the race.)

Lesson 14 Key Word Activity Master (see page 128)

Sample Answers:

1. Yes, the syllable is pronounced *lay* and gets the strongest beat.
2. Yes, because each person may sit beside any of nine others.
3. No, because friends should say favorable things about each other.
4. Yes, the people in a crowd may go their separate ways.
5. No, a temerarious person is bold.
6. No, the Eighteenth Amendment to the U.S. Constitution banning alcohol sales was repealed in 1933.
7. No, it has been treated to be hard.
8. No, he or she is not easily perturbed.
9. No, transmutation involves a physical change in state, such as copper pennies into gold.
10. Samples: Yes, to dress in an unconventional way, you would need to be reckless and unconcerned about rules. / No, it's possible to enjoy eccentric clothing and not be foolishly bold.
11. Samples: Yes, an ultimatum is a final, unchangeable demand. / No, sometimes people give an ultimatum but are secretly still willing to negotiate.
12. Samples: Yes, I like my water to be totally clear. / No, sometimes turbid water has sediments that make it cloudy, but it is still safe to drink.

ASSIGN Exercises

Book D, pages 129–132

REVIEW Lessons 13 and 14

Guide students in a game of Charades.

- Together, review the key words in Lessons 13 and 14 to list all the noun forms on slips of paper: *apostle, asterisk, constellation, cosmology, cosmopolite, epistle, insubordination, ordination, ordinance, rectitude, aspersion, dispersion, permutation, perturbation, temerarious, temerity, temperance, transmutation, ultimatum.*
- Give students time to try to memorize the listed words before the slips of paper are removed.
- Divide the group into two teams.
- Have one team member at a time choose a slip of paper, hold up fingers for the number of syllables, and pantomime the noun.
- Use a stopwatch to note the time it takes for teammates to guess the word. At the end of three minutes, if the team has not guessed, allow the other team one chance to guess the correct word.

SELECT Review Exercises

Book D, pages 133–136

LESSON 15

Literary and Historical References

2. temporal
The apostle Paul wrote letters of encouragement and advice to Christians in Corinth that included his reference to things temporal and eternal (Corinthians 4:18).

3. temporize
Anglo-Irish novelist Elizabeth Bowen (1899–1973) portrays an adolescent girl coming to terms with rejection in *The Death of the Heart* (1938).

Regarded as a superior military man, General George B. McClellan (1826–1885) nevertheless lost his command as general-in-chief of the Union Army to Ulysses S. Grant.

5. chronicle
Besides writing scholarly works, Oxford professor J(ohn) R(onald) R(euel) Tolkien (1892–1973) created a mythology that has become known around the world in *The Hobbit, The Lord of the Rings,* and *Silmarillion.*

10. superannuated
Mother Teresa, (1910–1997) born Agnes Gonxha Bojaxhiu in what became Yugoslavia, took holy orders and was a teacher in India before devoting her life to the needy, work which earned her the Nobel Peace Prize in 1979.

10. superannuated
Joseph Addison's reference to a "superannuated idol" appeared in the May 11, 1711, *Spectator.*

11. diurnal
Born in England, Anne Bradstreet (1612?–1672) lived most of her life in New England; her work shows the influence of earlier poets as well as of her immediate surroundings.

13. sojourn
English novelist Charlotte Brontë (1816–1855) uses her own experience as both student and teacher in a girls' school in Brussels for characters and atmosphere in *Villette.*

After the disastrous invasion of Russia in 1814, Napoleon Bonaparte (1769–1821) abdicated as emperor and was sent to Elba but returned to France, leading the army to defeat against English forces at Waterloo. Banished to St. Helena, he abdicated a second time and remained there until his death.

14. nocturne
In addition to nocturnes, Polish musician Frédéric Chopin (1810–1849) wrote concertos, preludes, mazurkas, and waltzes.

Exercise 15B, 1d   The observation by Henry David Thoreau (1817–1862) from the November, 1862, issue of the *Atlantic Monthly* reflects his interests as a philosopher, poet, and naturalist.

Exercise 15B, 4b   In Shakespeare's comedy *The Taming of the Shrew*, Bianca is free to marry when Petruchio's rough treatment tames Kate.

Exercise 15B, 5a   Diaries discovered in 1936 describe the hunger and hardship experienced by the Donner Party, the eighty-seven people who were trapped in Sierra Nevada snow storms in 1846 on their way to California.

Exercise 15B, 6b   Egyptian Queen Cleopatra (69–30 B.C.) was displaced as a sharer of her brother's throne but restored as queen by Julius Caesar.

Exercise 15B, 7b   A believer in states' rights, Confederate Mary Boykin Chesnut (1823– 1886) kept diaries during the Civil War, recording thoughts both personal and political.

Exercise 15B, 7c   Although many of the books of Annals have been lost, enough survive to show that Roman historian Livy (Titus Livius, 59 B.C.–A.D. 17) was impartial in assessing the fifteen-year war that Hannibal (247–183 B.C.) waged in Italy.

Exercise 15B, 8b   Although known chiefly for her fiction, Willa Cather (1873–1947) published a small book of poems, *April Twilights*, at her own expense in 1903.

Exercise 15C, 1   Born in New Zealand, Katherine Mansfield (1888–1923) is considered one of the founders of the modern short story form.

Exercise 15C, 3   As the conspirators plan the death of Caesar, Cassius says, "The clock hath stricken three," an anachronism since Caesar died on the Ides of March in 44 B.C. and standing clocks were not invented until the sixteenth century.

Exercise 15C, 4   Because Spanish chronicler Bernal Diaz (del Castillo) (1492–1568?) had himself fought in 110 battles and wished to tell a complete story of the Spanish conquest, he paid homage not only to Cortez, but also to soldiers, native people and customs, and the new world itself.

Exercise 15C, 6   *Dibs: In Search of Self* by Virginia M. Axline (b. 1911) tells of a psychotic young boy's journey to recovery.

Exercise 15C, 10   In addition to discovering the precession of the equinoxes and other planetary movements, Greek astronomer Hipparchus (160–125 B.C.) cataloged 1,080 stars and invented trigonometry.

Exercise 15C, 11	Edward Boykin is the compiler of this 1961 publication.
Exercise 15C, 12	In her films American actress Mae West (1893–1988) created a seductive persona and delivered numerous wisecracks.
Exercise 15D	Figures returning from history to celebrate the arrival of the new millennium are Leonardo da Vinci (1452–1519); Murasaki Shikibu (eleventh century); Nicolaus Copernicus (1473–1543); Galileo Galilei (1564–1642); and Karl Marx (1818– 1883).

INTRODUCE Lesson 15

(Book D, page 137)

Tell students that the theme of Lessons 15 and 16 is "Time."

Display, read, and translate this Latin expression (from page 137 of Lesson 15): *Carpe diem.* "Seize the day."

- Tell students that the original statement, by the Roman poet Horace, was longer: "Seize the day, put no trust in the morrow." Ask students what English-speakers mean when they use the Latin expression today. (Samples: Don't put off until tomorrow what you can do today./Live each day to the fullest.)

Ask: Which Latin word means "day"? (*diem*) Explain that English words based on the Latin root *dies* are among the words to learn in Lesson 15.

PREVIEW Familiar Words

(Book D, pages 137–140)

tempo, chronology, annual, diary, journal

ACTIVITY 1

The Latin *tempus* ("time") and related forms are sources of English words with the root *temp*. Help students think about the root meaning.

Display the familiar word *tempo*.

Have students demonstrate a fast tempo and a slow tempo.

Point out the root *temp*, explaining that this Latin root may be part of English words having to do with time.

ACTIVITY 2

The Greek *khronos* ("time") is the source of English words with the root *chron.* Help students think about the root meaning.

Display the familiar word *chronology.*

Have students create a timeline highlighting key milestones in their lives.

Point out the root *chron,* explaining that this Greek root appears in English words having to do with time.

ACTIVITY 3

The Latin *annus* ("year") is the source of English words with the root *ann(u)/enni.* Help students think about the root meaning.

Display the familiar word *annual.*

Ask: What are some *annual* events? (Samples: birthdays, many holidays, a county fair, graduation)

Tell students that *annual* is based on the Latin word for "year."

ACTIVITY 4

The Latin *dies* ("day") is the source of English words with the root *di(a)/jour.* Help students compare and contrast words with the root.

Display the familiar words *diary* and *journal.*

Ask: How are these words alike, and how are they different? (Samples: They are both daily records of events./They can both be personal./A *journal* is seen as more historical or objective./A *journal* also names a periodical.)

Tell students that both words are based on a Latin word for "day," but like most synonyms, they have taken different paths to enter English.

Have a student read aloud the dictionary derivations of *diary* and *journal* so that students can identify the word that came into English from Latin via Old French (journal; the word *journal* means "newspaper" in modern French).

ACTIVITY 5: Contrasting Roots

Have students tell whether they think the Latin root in *tempo* is the same as the Latin root in the Lesson 14 words *temper* and *temperance.* (No, the words *temper* and *temperance* come from the Latin root meaning "to combine in proportion"; *tempo* comes from a Latin root meaning "time.")

Offer this oral sentence, and have students tell how they can figure out a likely meaning of the emphasized word: *The classic period of Mayan civilization was contemporaneous with the decline of the Roman Empire.* (Sample: Contemporaneous events are happening at the same time; the context provides clues, along with knowing that the root *temp* can have to do with time. They might also know the word *contemporary.*)

ACTIVITY 6: Review Familiar Words

Review by having students name displayed words with roots meaning "time" ("tempo," "chronology"); "day" ("diary," "journal"); and "year" ("annual"). Lesson 15 also includes the Latin *nox* ("night") and related forms, which are sources of English words with the root *nox/noct.*

PRESENT Key Words

(Book D, pages 137–141)

Direct students to read the five roots and root families boldfaced on pages 137–141 of their Level D books. Then have them turn to page 137 to read the boxed key words chorally: *anachronism, annals, biennial, chronicle, diurnal, equinox, extempore, meridian, millennium, nocturne, sojourn, superannuated, synchronous, temporal, temporize.*

Present each key word by discussing the following:

- pronunciation
- definitions/connections to the root
- sentences
- parts of speech
- word forms

Use the *Nota Bene* with *temporal* to point out that students have learned two meanings for the root *temp*, as in *temper* and *temporal*. The word *temporal* is a homograph; its different meanings are based on different roots. Have a student read aloud both dictionary entries for *temporal.* Discuss what the Latin root is when *temporal* refers to bones of the skull. (The Latin root *tempus* mean "temple.")

Use the *Nota Bene* with *annals* to discuss this analogy:

annals : chronicles :: diary : journal. (Sample: The terms in both are nearly synonymous, but with slightly different shades of meaning. When differentiated, *annals* has a more historical connotation [i.e. events taking place outside the lifetime of the annalist]. Similarly, a *journal* takes a more objective look at events described by the journalist.)

Use the *Nota Bene* with *biennial* to encourage students to invent a mnemonic that will help them distinguish the confusables *biennial* and *biannual.* (Sample: a *biennial* happens every two years. A *biannual* always happens every year.)

Use the *Nota Bene* after *meridian* to ask students how remembering A.M. and P.M. will help them understand words that begin with *ante* and *post*, such as *antecedent* and *postoperative.* (Sample: The *ante* in A.M. means "before" and the *post* in P.M. means "after.") This meaning is also true in words such as *antecedent* ("preceding" in terms of grammar, math, or lineages) and *postoperative* (care "after" an operation).

Use the *Nota Bene* after *sojourn* to ask students to use *quotidian* as an adjective to describe several quotidian activities. (Samples: a *quotidian* evening of TV-watching; a *quotidian* bus ride to school; *quotidian* visits to the mall)

GUIDE Practice

Categories

Have students name the key word or words that belong in each list, and tell what the words have in common:

- sonata, concerto, étude, (nocturne; all are musical compositions)
- longitude, latitude, parallel, (meridian; all are imaginary measurements on the globe)
- antique, prehistoric, medieval, (superannuated; all describe things that come from the past)
- parallel, equivalent, analogous, (synchronous; all describe things that are alike)
- decade, era, century, (millennium; all name spans of years)
- register, journal, timeline, (chronicle, annals; all are records of events)
- evade, play for time, procrastinate, (temporize; all are delaying tactics)
- vacation, excursion, furlough, (sojourn; all name temporary visits or changes of routine)
- ad-libbed, improvised, unrehearsed, (extempore; all describe unplanned talks or performances)
- annual, weekly, hourly, (biennial, diurnal; all describe spans of time)
- season, solstice, ellipse, (equinox; all have to do with Earth's annual orbit around the sun)
- misstep, sour note, fish out of water, (anachronism; all are things that are out of place)
- fleeting, limited, finite, (temporal; all describe short periods of time)

Lesson 15 Key Word Activity Master (see page 129)

Answers:

1. the autumnal equinox
2. temporal matters
3. the annals of history
4. synchronous motion
5. a millennium
6. meridians
7. diurnal herbivores
8. a nocturne
9. an anachronism
10. a biennial chronicle
11. extemporaneous responses
12. a superannuated ordinance
13. a temporizing effort
14. attainment of the meridian
15. a chronicle of sojourns

ASSIGN Exercises

Book D, pages 142–145

LESSON 16

Literary and Historical References

5. neophyte

Adopting beliefs of Black Muslims while serving a prison term, black activist Malcolm X (1925–1965) had begun to form the Organization of Afro-American Unity when he was assassinated.

Founded by Italian nun Clare of Assisi (1194–1253) with the help of Saint Francis of Assisi, the society of Poor Clares is an austere community of cloistered nuns who renounce private property.

Americans Christine Evert Mill (b. 1954) and Czech-born Martina Navratilova (b. 1956) have won tennis titles at the Australian Women's Open, the French Open, Wimbledon, and the U.S. Open.

6. dour

In *Silas Marner* English novelist Mary Ann Evans (pseudonym George Eliot, 1819–1880) depicts a gruff recluse who warms to the baby girl left at his doorstep and becomes a doting father.

8. obdurate

In *David Copperfield* by Charles Dickens (1812–1870) the young David finds Aunt Betsey to be a fierce protector who ends the interview with Mr. Murdstone and his sister, "I'll knock your hat off and tread on it!"

English journalist Ian Fleming (1908–1964) has acquired loyal fans through spy novels and films that began in 1953 with the novel *Casino Royale*.

10. memoir

In *Memoirs of a Dutiful Daughter,* French author Simone de Beauvoir (1908–1986) shows in her early life the will to resist limits imposed by school and family on what girls may do and become.

14. senescent

In *Spoon River Anthology* by American author Edgar Lee Masters (1869–1950), Lucinda Matlock is one of the monologuists who reflect in turn on their regrets or satisfactions while they were alive in a small midwestern town.

15. surly

Having banished his one loyal daughter, King Lear laments the harsh treatment from Goneril and Regan, who send him out into a torrential rain storm and ultimately to his death in Shakespeare's tragedy *King Lear.*

Exercise 16B, 1b	Dame Margot Fonteyn (1919–1991), the prima ballerina of the Royal Ballet Company in London, became legendary for the grace and perfection of her art.
Exercise 16B, 2b	In stories, novels, and autobiography, African-American Zora Neale Hurston (1901–1960) dealt with customs and conflicts in the South.
Exercise 16B, 3a	Blue jeans have always been sturdy; in 1874 American clothing manufacturer Levi Strauss (1829–1902) began reinforcing seams with rivets.
Exercise 16B, 3b	Polish mathematician and scientist Benoit Mandelbrot (b. 1924), a believer in interdisciplinary studies, devised the theory of fractals: at all scales, shapes show the same pattern of roughness or irregularity.
Exercise 16B, 4d	American writer Harriet Beecher Stowe (1811–1896) wrote *Uncle Tom's Cabin, or Life among the Lowly* in 1852.
Exercise 16C, 2	The lively memoir of Nate Shaw, an illiterate black slave, was recorded in 1974 by historian Theodore Rosengarten as *All God's Dangers: the Life of Nate Shaw.*
Exercise 16C, 6	By the time Soviet agronomist Trofim Denisovich Lysenko (1898–1976) was removed from influence he had significantly slowed advancement of his country's science and agricultural development because of his early opposition to Mendelian theories of genetics.
Exercise 16C, 7	Methuselah's great age is cited in Genesis 5:27.
Exercise 16C, 9	The first chapter of *Great Expectations* by Charles Dickens (1812–1870) introduces Pip and the convict in their frightening encounter.
Exercise 16C, 10	American novelist Ken Kesey (1935–2001) used his experience as an attendant in a mental hospital in writing this novel.
Exercise 16C, 11	Soon after the opening of her own salon in Paris, French fashion designer Rose Bertin (1747–1813) received the patronage of Marie Antoinette, whose gowns made Mlle. Bertin famous and prosperous despite her condescending manner and even rude indifference to lesser patrons.

INTRODUCE Lesson 16

(Book D, page 146)

Remind students that the theme of Lessons 15 and 16 is "Time."

Display, read, and translate this Latin quotation (from page 146 of Lesson 16): *Senectus est natura loquacior.* "Old age is by nature more talkative."

- Ask students to identify any of the Latin words they can match to English ones. Students should recognize *natura* ("nature") and may recognize *loquacior* as containing the root *loquor* learned in Lesson 8, having to do with speaking.
- Point to *Senectus*—"old age"—telling students that words with the Latin root *sen* are among the words to learn in Lesson 16.

PREVIEW Familiar Words

(Book D, pages 146–149)

innovation, novelty, neon, memento, memorable, senate

ACTIVITY 1

The Latin *novus* ("new") is the source of English words with the root *nov*. Help students compare and contrast words with the root.

Display the familiar words *innovation* and *novelty*.

Read aloud each sentence with the emphasis shown, and direct students to complete it with one of the displayed words:

- Everyone likes novelty now and then because new experiences… (Sample: can be educational and exciting.)
- An example of an innovation that brought new ways of living is… (Samples: printing press, automobiles, the Internet)

Ask: What root appears in both words, and what does it mean? (The root *nov*, meaning "new.")

ACTIVITY 2

The Greek *neos* ("new") is the source of English words with the root *neo*. Help students make meaning connections.

Display the familiar word *neon*.

Tell students that the root *neo* comes from a Greek word meaning "new."

Ask: What might the meaning connection be between the Greek root and the English word? (Sample: The gas called neon seemed new when it was discovered.)

Explain that *neon* is an example of a *neologism*, a *new* word that people invent (students will learn *neologism* in the Key Words section of Lesson 16). When British chemists discovered a "new" element in 1898 they gave it the name *neon*, a form of the Greek root meaning "new."

ACTIVITY 3

The Latin *memoria* ("remembrance," "memory") is the source of English words with the root *mem*. Help students compare and contrast words with the root.

Display the familiar words *memento* and *memorable*.

Ask: What is a *memento*, and why might someone want a *memento* of a *memorable* event? (Sample: A *memento* is a souvenir or keepsake, and someone might want it as a reminder of a visit or celebration. A *memento* helps you *remember* the experience.)

Ask: What do you think the Latin root *mem* signals in words? (Sample: The meaning of the word may have to do with remembering.)

Explain the difference between *mem* in *memento* and *memorable*, and the root *mne* in *amnesia*. (Sample: The root *mne* is from the Greek. It means "mindful" as opposed to the Latin *mem* which means "remembrance, memory.")

ACTIVITY 4

The Latin *senescere* ("to grow old") and related forms are sources of English words with the root *sen*. Help students make meaning connections.

Display the familiar word *senate*.

Ask: What is a senate? (a body of lawmakers)

Tell students that in ancient Rome, the Senate was the governing council. Its name was based on a Latin word for "old" or "elders."

Ask: What meaning connection might there be between *senate* and *old*? (Sample: Age and wisdom go together; the members of a governing council are supposed to be wise elders.

ACTIVITY 5: Spelling Tip

Tell students that the word *memento* is often misspelled as *momento*. Discuss why knowing the root will help spellers avoid mistakes. (Sample: Knowing the root *mem* will help spellers avoid confusion.)

ACTIVITY 6: Review Familiar Words

Review by having students identify the root in each displayed word. Lesson 16 also includes the Latin *durare* ("to make hard," "to endure") and related forms, source of English words with the root *dur*; and *morari* ("to delay," "to loiter," "to tarry") and related forms, sources of English words with the root *mur/mor*.

PRESENT Key Words

(Book D, pages 146–149)

Direct students to read the six roots and root families boldfaced on pages 146–149 of their Level D books. Then have them turn to page 146 to read the boxed key words chorally: *demur, dour, duress, immemorial, memoir, memorabilia, moratorium, neoclassical, neologism, neophyte, nova, novice, obdurate, senescent, surly.*

Present each key word by discussing the following:

- pronunciation
- definitions/connections to the root
- sentences
- parts of speech
- word forms

Use the *Nota Bene* with *neoclassical* to discuss whether any local buildings reflect a *neoclassical* style. Have students draw a picture of a building demonstrating neoclassical style. (Sample: the drawing might have Greek columns or a domed roof)

GUIDE Practice

Cause and Effect

Have students complete each sentence:

- A confession extracted under *duress* is not valid because (Sample: the accused person may have only confessed to escape the harsh treatment.)

- A nation might request a *moratorium* on paying its debts to other countries because (Sample: it needs more time to improve its economy and raise the money it borrowed.)

- Baseball *memorabilia* are popular because (Sample: lovers of the sport like to connect with great teams of the past by collecting cards, signed balls, photos, and other items.)

- A *nova* is of scientific interest because (Sample: a sudden and dramatic change in the brightness of a star offers astrophysicists opportunities to learn about stellar energy and matter.)

- A *neophyte* might need help using a computer because (Sample: he or she is learning a new skill.)

- Tightly closed lips contribute to a *dour* expression because (Sample: they make a person's face look stern and mean. Have students demonstrate.)

- *Senescence* is a time for reflection because (Sample: older people can think about the long lives they have led.)

- Examples of *neologisms* related to computers are (Samples: email, spam, surf, hack, bug, blog.)

- Certain forms of architecture, painting, and literature are called *neoclassical* because (Sample: they are a revival of the styles of classical Greece and Rome.)

- Every professional athlete was once a *novice* because (Sample: everyone had to learn the sport and did not start out with expertise.)

- A person who is nominated for an office might *demur* because (Sample: he or she doesn't want the post.)

- A store with *surly* salesclerks is unlikely to prosper because (Sample: customers who are treated impolitely won't come back.)

- Sometimes it is necessary to be *obdurate* because (Sample: you have to stand up for your beliefs.)

- Prehistory is *immemorial* because (Sample: there are no written records.)

- A *memoir* is considered nonfiction because (Sample: the writer is telling about real-life events.)

Lesson 16 Key Word Activity Master (see page 130)

Answers:

1. neoclassical
2. neologism
3. neophyte
4. surly
5. nova
6. senescent
7. obdurate
8. memoir
9. memorabilia
10. immemorial
11. novice
12. demur
13. duress
14. dour
15. moratorium

ASSIGN Exercises

Book D, pages 149–153

REVIEW Lessons 15 and 16

Guide students in a quiz-show–style game of What's My Word?

- Divide the group into teams of three or four players.
- For each round of play, one team sits on the panel.
- The student game-show host reads a random context sentence from Lesson 15 or 16, substituting *blank* for the target word.
- Team members confer to name the word. They earn a point for each correctly named word, but lose their turn as panelists if they make an error.
- Continue until all teams have had at least one chance to sit on the panel.
- Help students create new context sentences.

SELECT Review Exercises

Book D, pages 153–156

Lesson 1 Key Word Activity Master

Name _____ Date _____

Decode the Message

Choose the word that fits in the sentence, then circle the letter beside it.

1. The ancient Greeks' woodland gods reveal the culture's ___.

   theocracy   **s**
   pantheism   **t**
   apotheosis   **u**

2. Schools must meet requirements for ___.

   accreditation   **h**
   credulity   **i**
   pantheon   **j**

3. The witnesses agreed, which added ___ to the report.

   divinity   **d**
   credence   **e**
   theology   **f**

4. Seers claim to ___ the future.

   credence   **m**
   accredit   **n**
   divine   **o**

5. Some sports fans seem to ___ the players.

   divinity   **a**
   deity   **b**
   deify   **c**

6. International ___ gathered to discuss the world's religions.

   theologians   **r**
   pantheists   **s**
   atheists   **t**

7. The believers held firmly to their ___.

   creed   **a**
   atheism   **b**
   apotheosis   **c**

8. A(n) ___ would believe strongly in the separation of church and state.

   divinity   **r**
   apotheosis   **s**
   atheist   **t**

9. A(n) ___ person is easily tricked.

   credulous   **i**
   accredited   **j**
   creditable   **k**

10. Zeus and Jupiter were comparable ___.

    theocracies   **a**
    patheons   **b**
    deities   **c**

11. The spiritual leader attended a school of ___.

    divinity   **a**
    credence   **b**
    theocracy   **c**

12. The Norse ___ included Thor, the god of thunder.

    pantheon   **l**
    divine   **m**
    pantheists   **n**

13. The gymnast performed ___ in her first competition.

    credulously   **j**
    incredulously   **k**
    creditably   **k**

14. This grand painting is the ___ of group portraits.

    pantheon   **x**
    apotheosis   **y**
    divinity   **z**

15. Write the circled letters in order on the line below to answer this question: *When religious leaders govern, how is the nation ruled?*

_____

   115

Lesson 2 Key Word Activity Master

Name _____ Date _____

What Do You Call It?

Underline the answer to each question.

1. What do you call apologies for harmful actions?
   attempts to expiate   execrable language

2. What do you call complete dedication to a cause?
   consecration   sacrilege

3. What do you call complete dedication to a religious life?
   a sanction   piety

4. What do you call earnings of ten cents per hour?
   a pittance   an impious amount

5. What do you call a place to feel safe?
   sanctity   a sanctuary

6. What do you call a play that the authorities have approved?
   a sanctioned performance   a hierarchical drama

7. What do you call an attitude of superiority?
   a sanctimonious manner   sacrilege

8. What do you call the chief executive of a business?
   the top of the hierarchy   first of the hieroglyphs

9. What do you call disrespectful treatment of holy objects?
   sacramental behavior   impious behavior

10. What do you call Grandpa's beloved armchair that nobody else can use?
    his sanctimonious spot   his sacrosanct spot

11. What do you call the writings of ancient Egyptians?
    a hieroglyphic system   a hierarchical system

12. What do you call a church, temple, or mosque?
    a building for sacrilege   a place of sanctity

13. What do you call priestly garments?
    sanctimonious dress   sacramental robes

14. What do you call the destruction of a holy center?
    an execrable sacrilege   an expiated consecration

Lesson 3 Key Word Activity Master

Name _____ Date _____

Letter Clues

Choose the key word that matches each clue, and write it letter by letter.
(Some letters will be within parentheses.)

agnostic	dogmatic	physiognomy
amnesty	frenetic	prognosis
arraign	heterodox	rationale
criterion	hypocrisy	rationalize
dogma	mnemonic	schizophrenia

Clues

1. antonym for *calm*   — (—) — — — — — —

2. absolute truth   — — — — (—)

3. synonym for *nonconforming*   — — (—) — — — — — —

4. describes a rigid viewpoint   — — — — — — (—) —

5. a person who questions belief   — — — (—) — — — —

6. a rhyme can be one   — (—) — — — — — —

7. do this before deciding to have a trial   (—) — — — — — —

8. underlying cause or reason   — — — — — — — (—) —

9. quality related to dishonesty   — — — — — — (—) — —

10. a mental illness   — — — — (—) — — — — — — — —

11. synonym for *pardon*   (—) — — — — — —

12. to justify, often for selfish reasons   — — (—) — — — — — — — —

13. a "cruel" chin might be part of this   — — — — (—) — — — — — —

14. a kind of prediction   — — — — — (—) — — —

15. a requirement   — — — — — — — — (—)

Answer this question by writing the parenthetical letters above on the line below: *Explaining that you eat sweets because they give you quick energy is an example of what kind of reasoning?*

16. _____

Lesson 4 Key Word Activity Master

Name _____ Date _____

Sentence Pairs

Choose the key word that fits in both sentences.

cognition	impute	putative
cognizant	notorious	repute
compute	plebiscite	sagacious
connoisseur	presage	sage
conscientious	prescience	sapient

1. _____
The student is ___ about completing homework.
Protests against injustice are ___ actions.

2. _____
The ___ expressed the citizens' views.
Vote on the issue when the ___ is held.

3. _____
Reasoning and using judgment are features of ___.
Psychologists use tests to measure learning and ___.

4. _____
The townspeople seeking advice visited the ___.
In folklore, owls may represent ___ elders.

5. _____
The candidates tried to ___ dishonesty to one another.
It is easy to ___ faults to those you dislike.

6. _____
Vitamin C is a ___ preventive for colds.
The ___ author of the work may have actually employed a ghostwriter.

7. _____
A solar eclipse was considered a ___ of terrible things to come.
A sudden end to birds' songs may ___ a storm.

8. _____
Captain Teach, known as Blackbeard, was a ___ pirate.
My sister is ___ for her practical jokes.

9. _____
He proceeded, not ___ of the hazards.
Try to be ___ of others' viewpoints.

10. _____
A ___ question reveals clear thinking.
With ___ leadership, this business will prosper.

11. _____
The woman is a ___ of fine food.
The art ___ collects modern paintings.

12. _____
Nobody has great ___ about what the stock market will do.
Having what you need for any emergency requires ___.

13. _____
This school is held in high ___.
She was ___ ed to be a spy.

14. _____
A ___ judge of character, the man knew who could and could not be trusted.
A sagacious person is likely to be ___.

15. Find the one word in the box that you did not use. Write two sentences with it.
_____
_____

Lesson 5 Key Word Activity Master

Name _____ Date _____

Choice Words

Circle the word in parentheses that fits in the sentence.

1. When Hank was told to "Keep the secret under your hat," his (literal/literate) interpretation caused him to reply, "But I'm not wearing a hat."

2. Tongue twisters such as *She sells seashells by the seashore* use (onomatopoeia/alliteration).

3. When the company president wrote an editorial for the newspaper, he used the (acronym/pseudonym) I. M. Rich.

4. After the cheating was exposed, the athlete's promising career came to a sudden and (ignominious/literate) end.

5. The familiar plant called a dandelion is identified as *Taraxacum officinale* in scientific (nomenclature/conscription).

6. "I refuse to (subscribe/proscribe) to the notion that physics is too difficult for some students," said the science teacher.

7. The disappearance of certain birds from the region is (ascribed/circumscribed) to their loss of habitat.

8. Words such as *sizzle* and *clunk* are examples of (obliteration/onomatopoeia).

9. When coffee was spilled on the notepad, the important message was (circumscribed/obliterated).

10. Immigrants to the United States who are (literate/transcribed) in their native languages do not necessarily know how to read and write English.

11. In an all-volunteer army, there are no (pseudonyms/conscripts).

12. An abbreviation, such as TV or USA, is slightly different from an (acronym/alliteration) such as AWOL—"absent without leave"—which is pronounced like a word.

13. The youth center posted a long list of rules and (proscriptions/ascriptions), with the main purpose of promoting safety and respect.

14. Imaginary lines of longitude cross both poles as they (circumscribe/subscribe) the globe.

15. The reporter (transcribed/literalized) the interview from a taped recording.

Lesson 6 Key Word Activity Master

Name _____ Date _____

Yes or No?

Read each question. Circle *Y* for *Yes* or *N* for *No*, and then write the reason for your choice.

1. Can a spoken account be graphic? **Y N**

   _____

2. Can you find an epigraph in your *Vocabulary from Classical Roots* book? **Y N**

   _____

3. Is choreography performed by an orchestra? **Y N**

   _____

4. Are analogous situations comparable? **Y N**

   _____

5. Can a map show topography? **Y N**

   _____

6. Should an apologist speak forcefully? **Y N**

   _____

7. Could a logo be a written paragraph? **Y N**

   _____

8. Is your state representative known as an eclectic official? **Y N**

   _____

9. Is a lexicon a kind of dictionary? **Y N**

   _____

10. Are details trivial in logistics? **Y N**

    _____

11. Is an epilogue the same as a eulogy? **Y N**

    _____

12. Could graffiti show an epigram? **Y N**

    _____

13. Is a lithographer a graphic artist? **Y N**

    _____

Lesson 7 Key Word Activity Master

Name _____ Date _____

Letter Clues

Choose the key word that matches each clue, and write it letter by letter.
(Some letters will be within parentheses.)

affable	edict	interdiction
dictatorial	gloss	jurisdiction
diction	indict	malediction
dictum	indite	polyglot
ditty	ineffable	valediction

Clues

1. synonym for *decree*   — — — (—) —

2. in a domineering manner   — — — — — — — (—) — — —

3. to write with careful consideration   — (—) — — — —

4. "Row, Row, Row Your Boat,"   — — (—) — —
   for example

5. a city, to its police chief   — — (—) — — — — — — — —

6. describes an easygoing person   — — — (—) — — —

7. a farewell oration   — — — — — (—) — — — — —

8. refusal to permit   — — — — — — (—) — — — —

9. do this after the arraignment   — — — — — (—) —

10. this is like a proverb   — — — (—) — —

11. word choice   — — — — (—) — —

12. speaker of many tongues   — — — — — — (—) —

13. synonym for *sacred*   — (—) — — — — — — —

14. this is like a footnote   — — — (—) —

15. antonym for *blessing*   — — — — — — — — — — —

Answer this question by writing the parenthetical letters above on the line below:
People who give maledictions followed by benedictions are sending what kinds of messages?

16. _____

121

Lesson 8 Key Word Activity Master

Name _____ Date _____

Sentence Pairs

Choose the key word that fits in both sentences.

acclamation	forensic	locution
circumlocution	forum	loquatious
clamor	lingo	proverbial
colloquium	lingua franca	verbatim
declaim	linguist	verbose

1. _____
   Memorize the story to retell it ___.
   The ___ account shows exactly what
   the speaker said.

2. _____
   Traders from different cultures used
   a(n) ___ to communicate.
   The ___ was a mix of three languages.

3. _____
   With the company losing money, the
   ___ rats are deserting the sinking ship.
   Due to their ___ curiosity, young
   children frequently begin questions
   with why.

4. _____
   The ___ talk-show host gave the guests
   almost no opportunity to speak.
   Shy and silent at first, the kindergartner
   later became surprisingly ___.

5. _____
   Say the poem naturally; do not ___ it.
   To ___ well, project your voice.

6. _____
   Adults often can't understand the ___
   of teenagers.
   Every field of study has its own ___.

7. _____
   A slang ___ is unsuitable for a term
   paper.
   An idiom such as *skeleton in the closet* is
   a figurative ___.

8. _____
   A crime lab specializes in ___ science.
   The school was famous for its ___
   team, which won debating awards.

9. _____
   Voters may ___ for change.
   It was difficult to hear the teacher
   through the ___ of students in the
   hallway.

10. _____
    The ___ is studying Cherokee grammar.
    A skilled ___, the man worked as a
    translator.

11. _____
    The library sponsors a monthly ___
    on political issues.
    Your voice can be heard if you
    participate in the forum or ___.

12. _____
    "Omit needless words," advised a
    famous teacher who warned against
    ___ writing.
    After listening to the ___ instructions,
    I was thoroughly confused.

13. _____
    The interviewee avoided answering the
    questions by using one ___ after
    another.
    Write clearly and briefly, without ___.

14. _____
    The Internet is a global ___ for
    everyone with an opinion to express.
    Goods were sold at the ___.

15. Find the one word that you did not use. On another sheet of paper, write two
    sentences with it.

Lesson 9 Key Word Activity Master

Name _____ Date _____

Decode the Message

Choose the word that fits in the sentence, then circle the letter beside it.

1. Tiles made of ___ surround the fireplace.

rustic	l
terra cotta	m
humus	n

2. Sheepdogs were bred for ___ work.

paramount	c
mountebank	d
pastoral	e

3. A tomb is a place of ___.

interment	d
exhumation	e
rusticity	f

4. Pioneers built ___ homes from logs.

rustic	i
rusticate	j
terrestrial	k

5. The ___ was a smooth talker who fooled many people.

humus	s
mountebank	t
promontory	u

6. The moon is nearest Earth at its ___.

perigee	e
apogee	f
terrestrial	g

7. Rotting leaves contribute ___ to soil.

terrestrial	p
rusticity	q
humus	r

8. Some city children go to summer camp to ___ for several weeks.

rusticate	r
exhume	s
pastoral	t

9. Unlike ___ plants, tropical orchids grow on other plants, not in soil.

terrestrial	a
geocentric	b
humus	c

10. The ___ feature of a democracy is government by the citizens themselves.

paramount	n
mountebank	o
geocentric	p

11. The culture of ancient Athens reached its ___ during the "golden age" of Pericles.

perigee	d
apogee	e
promontory	f

12. After cooking together all day, may family shared a wonderful ___.

repast	a
promontory	b
perigee	c

13. Scientists use sound waves to collect ___ data.

humus	m
geocentric	n
apogee	o

14. At the edge of the ___ is a sheer drop to the sea.

terrestrial	c
interment	d
promontory	e

15. The cause of death was determined after the body was ___.

exhumed	a
interred	b
perigee	c

16. Write the circled letters in order on the blanks below to answer this question: What large body of water has a name that means "middle of land"?

__ __ __ __ __ __ __ __ __ __ __ __ __ __ __ __ __ S __ __

Lesson 10 Key Word Activity Master

Name _____ Date _____

What Do You Call It?

Underline the answer to each question.

1. What do you call the sudden inspiration to write a great poem?
   an aspirated moment   an epiphany

2. What do you call the feeling that nothing can go right?
   a phantasmic mood   a dispirited condition

3. What do you call an unnatural kind of breathing?
   hyperventilation   aspiration

4. What do you call the material used in a translucent scarf?
   diaphanous fabric   sycophancy

5. What do you call the force that leads to courageous actions?
   the animus to heroism   pusillanimous aspiration

6. What do you call the characteristic of remaining calm in an emergency?
   equanimity   hyperventilation

7. What do you call a strange creature that appears in a dream?
   an ethereal animus   a phantasm

8. What do you call a heavenly region?
   the ether   the epiphany

9. What do you call the figurative expression *It's raining buckets*?
   hyperbole   a phantasm

10. What do you call the breath you see on a very cold day?
    hyperborean aspiration   an etherized hyperventilation

11. What do you call expressing hatred by shouting and fist-shaking?
    aspiring to an ethereal state   venting one's animus

12. What do you call a servile and cowardly flatterer?
    a dispirited aspirant   a pusillanimous sycophant

13. What do you call an astronaut's hopes and dreams?
    ethereal aspirations   diaphanous equanimity

Lesson 11 Key Word Activity Master

Name _____ Date _____

Synonym Replacement

Choose a key word that could replace the boldfaced word or words without changing the meaning of the sentence.

caustic	flagrant	pyre
cauterize	flamboyant	pyromania
conflagration	incendiary	pyrotechnics
effervescent	incense	scintilla
fervid	inflammatory	scintillate

1. _____
   Everyone oohed and aahed at the display of **fireworks.**

2. _____
   Unfairness may **infuriate** the people who are victims.

3. _____
   Showing **outright** disobedience, the student refused to take his seat.

4. _____
   The medic knew how to **sear** the wound to prevent infection.

5. _____
   "You will find not one **iota** of evidence against me," said the suspect.

6. _____
   My sister attracts friends with her enthusiastic manner and **bubbly** personality.

7. _____
   Her **inflammatory** comments caused a stir in the audience.

8. _____
   The performers wore **showy** costumes and tall hats with pink plumes.

9. _____
   The boy's **sarcastic** comment was more hurtful than witty.

10. _____
    The singer's magnificent voice is sure to **glitter** as brilliantly as her diamond necklace.

11. _____
    The shipwrecked sailors tended the **bonfire,** hoping it would be seen from afar.

12. _____
    The authorities viewed him as a troublemaker who made **incendiary** remarks.

13. _____
    An undoused campfire led to a **fire that spread through acres of forest.**

14. _____
    The **psychological problem of fire-setting** is similar to other compulsions.

15. _____
    Some of the most **zealous** supporters of the candidate volunteered more than fifteen hours a day.

Lesson 12 Key Word Activity Master

Name _____ Date _____

Choice Words

Circle the word in parentheses that fits in the sentence.

1. We relaxed in the boat, enjoying the restful (undulations/inundations) of the water.

2. According to the recipe, the fish should soak in the (marinade/effluence) for an hour.

3. They had more money than they could possibly need, but were (cormorants/naves) in their business dealings.

4. The garbage truck overturned, and for days afterward the smell (dehydrated/nauseated) everyone in the neighborhood.

5. The (pontification/pontiff) is the leader of Roman Catholics worldwide.

6. The cynical saying, "No good deed goes unpunished" describes generous efforts that (redound/inundate) in negative ways.

7. Because all gifts are free, advertisements that offer "free gifts" contain a (redundancy/pontification).

8. The ways in which water collects underground is part of a region's (effluence/hydrology).

9. Because water trade has always been important to human settlement, cities are likely to be found at the (confluence/flux) of two or more rivers.

10. Drink plenty of water on hot days to avoid (hydrology/dehydration).

11. After a week of steady rain, the (marinade/effluent) from the river had poured into the streets.

12. After finishing her CPR course, the girl put an ad in the newspaper offering her babysitting service, and was soon (undulated/inundated) with calls.

13. A successful inventor has an endless (inundate/flux) of ideas.

14. Speakers who (marinate/pontificate) tend to annoy or bore their listeners.

15. The largest area in a church is the (pontiff/nave).

Lesson 13 Key Word Activity Master

Name _____ Date _____

Decode the Message

Choose the word that fits in the sentence, then circle the letter beside it.

1. Seven stars in the ___ Ursa Major are called the Big Dipper.

constellation	a
cosmology	b
cosmopolitan	c

2. The town has an ___ against noise.

epistle	r
ordinance	s
insubordinate	t

3. "I never lie," he said, proud of his ___.

rectitude	t
insubordination	u
ordination	v

4. How can we ___ this injustice?

asterisk	p
insubordinate	q
rectify	r

5. The journalists known as muckrakers were ___ for reforms in industry.

epistles	n
apostles	o
deify	p

6. A(n) ___ performance deserves a standing ovation.

stolid	n
inordinate	o
stellar	p

7. The guard stood silently and ___.

inordinately	f
cosmologically	g
stolidly	h

8. Pen pals have a(n) ___ relationship.

rectitude	w
inordinate	x
epistolary	y

9. A note explains why some items in the list are ___.

asterisked	s
constellations	t
astral	u

10. Obedience was rewarded; ___ was punished.

cosmology	h
insubordination	i
rectitude	j

11. A cabinet full of disinfectants revealed her ___ obsession with cleanliness.

astral	a
cosmopolitan	b
inordinate	c

12. Immigrants from all over the world settled in this ___ city.

epistolary	h
cosmopolitan	i
rectified	j

13. Ancient astrologers interpreted ___ messages.

astral	s
apostolic	t
cosmopolite	u

14. "We the people ... do ___ and establish this Constitution for the United States of America."

rectify	s
ordain	t
asterisk	u

15. The ___ explained the movements of galaxies.

cosmology	s
stellar	t
ordination	u

16. Write the circled letters in order, and find the answer to this question: *Who are the scientific experts on cosmological questions?* _____

Lesson 14 Key Word Activity Master

Name _____ Date _____

Yes or No

Read each question. Circle *Y* for *Yes* or *N* for *No*, and then write the reason for your choice.

1. When the word *constellation* is said, is the penultimate syllable stressed? **Y N**

   _____

2. Are permutations involved in seating ten guests at a table? **Y N**

   _____

3. Should friends cast aspersions on each other's loyalty? **Y N**

   _____

4. Can a crowd disperse? **Y N**

   _____

5. Is timidity a feature of a temerarious temperament? **Y N**

   _____

6. Were supporters of temperance ultimately successful in their goal? **Y N**

   _____

7. Does tempered glass break easily? **Y N**

   _____

8. Is an imperturbable person quick to anger? **Y N**

   _____

9. Is exchanging ten pennies for a dime an example of transmutation? **Y N**

   _____

10. Would it require temerity to wear outré fashions? **Y N**

   _____

11. Is an ultimatum immutable? **Y N**

   _____

12. Would drinking turbid water perturb you? **Y N**

   _____

Lesson 15 Key Word Activity Master

Name _____ Date _____

What Do You Call It?

Underline the answer to each question.

1. What do you call the beginning of fall in the Northern Hemisphere?
   the autumnal equinox   the annual synchrony

2. What do you call everyday concerns?
   temporal matters   extempore problems

3. What do you call a timeline of major events of the past?
   an anachronistic account   the annals of history

4. What do you call a dance in which partners mirror each other's movements?
   an equinoctial performance   synchronous motion

5. What do you call a time span of ten centuries?
   superannuation   a millennium

6. What do you call the divisions that determine time zones?
   meridians   equinoxes

7. What do you call animals that graze during the day and sleep at night?
   diurnal herbivores   temporizing herds

8. What do you call a musical composition that conveys a dreamy mood?
   a nocturne   a diurnal sojourn

9. What do you call a typewriter in a modern office?
   a superannuated annal   an anachronism

10. What do you call a periodical published every other year?
    a biennial chronicle   a diurnal journal

11. What do you call an interviewee's answers to unexpected questions?
    synchronized replies   extemporaneous responses

12. What do you call a city law that requires a bathroom for every three dwellings?
    a superannuated ordinance   an extempore anachronism

13. What do you call a plan to make a plan?
    a temporizing effort   an extempore attempt

14. What do you call a peak performance by an athlete?
    attainment of the meridian   an extemporary feat

15. What do you call a traveler's diary?
    temporizing annals   a chronicle of sojourns

Lesson 16 Key Word Activity Master

Name _____ Date _____

Synonym Replacement

Choose a key word that could replace the boldfaced word or words without changing the meaning of the sentence.

demur	memorabilia	nova
dour	moratorium	novice
duress	neoclassical	obdurate
immemorial	neologism	senescent
memoir	neophyte	surly

1. _____
   The house is in the **Greek Revival** style.

2. _____
   The word *gas* was a **coinage** based on the Greek *chaos*.

3. _____
   The **beginner** soon felt comfortable in her advanced aerobics class.

4. _____
   She sneered and made a **gruff** remark.

5. _____
   When ancient people saw a(n) **stellar explosion,** they thought it was a new star.

6. _____
   The **aging** teacher contemplated his retirement.

7. _____
   Facts and evidence won't change an opinion held by a(n) **stubborn** mind.

8. _____
   His **autobiography** told of growing up in simpler times.

9. _____
   The state representative has a collection of **souvenirs** from her political campaigns.

10. _____
   These tales have **ancient** roots and no known authors.

11. _____
   I'm just a(n) **neophyte** at carpentry, and can build only simple things.

12. _____
   The coach wanted to **object,** but knew she would have to give a speech at the awards ceremony.

13. _____
   They signed the contract because of **threats and pressure.**

14. _____
   His **gloomy** facial expression displayed his unhappiness.

15. _____
   The lawmakers voted for a two-year **delay** before considering the construction project.

Answers to Exercises

LESSON 1

EXERCISE 1A

1. d
2. b
3. d
4. d
5. d
6. b
7. b
8. c
9. e
10. a
11. a
12. d
13. e

EXERCISE 1B

1. b
2. a
3. c
4. d
5. d

EXERCISE 1C

1. credulous
2. Pantheon
3. creed
4. deified or apotheosized
5. theology
6. theocracy
7. pantheistic
8. credence
9. atheist
10. apotheosis or deification
11. creditable

EXERCISE 1D

1. deities or divinities
2. deified or apotheosized
3. deities or divinities
4. pantheon
5. creed
6. pantheism
7. theology
8. accredited

LESSON 2

EXERCISE 2A

1. e
2. e
3. b
4. d
5. c
6. d
7. b
8. b
9. c
10. a
11. c
12. c
13. e

EXERCISE 2B

1. d
2. d
3. b
4. a
5. a
6. c

EXERCISE 2C

1. hierarchy
2. piety
3. sacrosanct
4. sacramental
5. hieroglyphic
6. sanctimonious
7. expiate
8. sacreligious or impious
9. execrate
10. pittance
11. sanctity

EXERCISE 2D

1. hierarchy
2. sanctioned
3. execrated
4. consecrated
5. sacrament
6. sacrilege

REVIEW EXERCISES FOR LESSONS 1 AND 2

EXERCISE 1

1. d
2. a
3. b
4. a

EXERCISE 2

1. D
2. F
3. E
4. G
5. H
6. I
7. A
8. C
9. B
10. J

EXERCISE 3

a. apotheosis
b. deity
c. execrated
d. expiate
e. deified
f. pantheon

a. theocracy
b. sanctions
c. atheists
d. impious

LESSON 3

EXERCISE 3A	EXERCISE 3B	EXERCISE 3C	EXERCISE 3D
1. c	1. a	1. mnemonic	1. heterodox
2. a	2. c	2. amnesty	2. dogmatic
3. a	3. d	3. schizophrenia	3. arraigned
4. d	4. c	4. rationalized	4. rationalizing
5. b	5. b	5. agnostic	5. hypocrisy
6. b	6. c	6. rationale	6. schizophrenia
7. c	7. b	7. physiognomy	7. criteria or
8. b	8. d	8. dogma	rationale
9. a	9. a	9. criterion	
10. b			
11. c			
12. c			

LESSON 4

EXERCISE 4A	EXERCISE 4B	EXERCISE 4C	EXERCISE 4D
1. e	1. a	1. computed	1. putative
2. a	2. d	2. repute	2. cognition or
3. c	3. c	3. sagacity	cognizance
4. b	4. d	4. plebiscite	3. compute
5. e	5. a	5. imputes	4. cognizant
6. b	6. b	6. conscientious	5. notorious
7. c	7. c	7. cognition	6. conscientious
8. a	8. c	8. presages	
9. a	9. d	9. notorious	
10. e		10. sapience	
		11. sage	

REVIEW EXERCISES FOR LESSONS 3 AND 4

EXERCISE 1	EXERCISE 2	EXERCISE 3
1. e	1. J	a. rationale
2. d	2. H	b. notorious
3. e	3. I	c. cognizant
4. d	4. D	d. conscientiously
5. e	5. F	e. criterion
	6. G	f. reputed
	7. B	
	8. E	a. dogma
	9. A	b. heterodox
	10. C	c. imputed
		d. hypocrisy

LESSON 5

EXERCISE 5A

1. b
2. d
3. d
4. d
5. c
6. c
7. a
8. a
9. a
10. d

EXERCISE 5B

1. d
2. d
3. d
4. d
5. c
6. a
7. d
8. a

EXERCISE 5C

1. alliteration
2. conscripted
3. onomatopoeia
4. literally
5. ascribed
6. ignominious
7. pseudonym
8. subscribe
9. nomenclature
10. transcribed
11. acronym
12. obliterated

EXERCISE 5D

1. word for word
2. written-out or copied
3. encircled
4. prohibited
5. confined or enclosed
6. denounced or condemned
7. assented

LESSON 6

EXERCISE 6A

1. e
2. e
3. a
4. c
5. b
6. e
7. b
8. e
9. b
10. d
11. a

EXERCISE 6B

1. a
2. d
3. d
4. a
5. c
6. a
7. d
8. c
9. a

EXERCISE 6C

1. Graffiti
2. graphic
3. epigraph
4. choreography
5. lithograph
6. lexicon
7. epilogue
8. analogy
9. logistics
10. logo
11. epigram

EXERCISE 6D

1. varied
2. dance composer
3. visual or pictorial
4. symbolic design
5. services and supplies
6. Apologists
7. topography
8. eclectic
9. analogies

REVIEW EXERCISES FOR LESSONS 5 AND 6

EXERCISE 1

1. b
2. d
3. a
4. b
5. b

EXERCISE 2

1. G
2. H
3. B
4. J
5. C
6. E
7. D
8. F
9. I
10. A

EXERCISE 3

a. graphically
b. logos
c. acronyms
d. alliterate

a. circumscribed
b. literate
c. conscripts
d. ignominy
e. lexicon
f. graffiti

LESSON 7

EXERCISE 7A
1. b   12. a
2. c   13. e
3. d
4. d
5. b
6. c
7. a
8. b
9. b
10. c
11. c

EXERCISE 7B
1. b
2. c
3. c
4. a
5. a
6. d
7. b

EXERCISE 7C
1. affable
2. ditty
3. jurisdiction
4. maledictions
5. dictatorial
6. indite
7. diction
8. dictum or edict
9. polyglots
10. interdiction

EXERCISE 7D
1. indescribable or inexpressible
2. word choice
3. explanation
4. farewell
5. composed or written
6. authoritative opinions
7. friendly
8. prohibitions

LESSON 8

EXERCISE 8A
1. b
2. a
3. c
4. a
5. c
6. c
7. a
8. a
9. c
10. e

EXERCISE 8B
1. b
2. d
3. d
4. d
5. c
6. a
7. b

EXERCISE 8C
1. verbatim
2. lingua franca
3. colloquium
4. circumlocution
5. locutions
6. forum
7. lingo
8. loquacious
9. linguists
10. declaim
11. forensic
12. clamor
13. verbose

EXERCISE 8D
1. debating
2. polyglots
3. roundabout expressions
4. open discussion
5. enthusiastic approval
6. noisy or exclamatory
7. well-known
8. proverb-like or traditional

REVIEW EXERCISES FOR LESSONS 7 AND 8

EXERCISE 1
1. d
2. a
3. a
4. d

EXERCISE 2
1. farewell
2. for word
3. excessive or too many
4. blessing
5. write
6. prohibition or proscription
7. praise or approval
8. choice or use
9. authority
10. cursing

EXERCISE 3
a. jurisdiction
b. indicted
c. clamor
d. acclaimed

a. forum
b. loquacious
c. affable
d. verbose
e. gloss
f. ineffable

LESSON 9

EXERCISE 9A

1. e
2. a
3. c
4. a
5. d
6. b
7. c
8. e
9. d
10. c
11. b

EXERCISE 9B

1. c
2. d
3. b
4. b
5. c
6. c
7. c
8. a

EXERCISE 9C

1. mountebanks
2. paramount
3. repast
4. geocentric
5. rusticate
6. perigee, apogee
7. humus
8. promontories
9. exhumed, interred
10. terra cotta

EXERCISE 9D

1. apex or high point
2. idealized rural scene
3. country or rural people
4. earthbound or earthly
5. reddish brown
6. go to the country
7. rough or unrefined
8. unearthed or disinterred or brought to light

LESSON 10

EXERCISE 10A

1. d
2. d
3. c
4. e
5. c
6. d
7. b
8. b
9. c
10. a
11. e
12. b

EXERCISE 10B

1. b
2. c
3. d
4. c
5. c
6. d
7. d

EXERCISE 10C

1. dispirited
2. hyperborean
3. pusillanimous
4. phantasm
5. sycophants
6. hyperbole(s)
7. hyperventilation
8. aspirate
9. equanimity
10. ether
11. epiphany

EXERCISE 10D

1. ether
2. hyperborean
3. hyperventilation
4. phantasm
5. ethereal
6. equanimity
7. aspiration
8. epiphany
9. animus

REVIEW EXERCISES FOR LESSONS 9 AND 10

EXERCISE 1

1. d
2. c
3. c
4. e
5. c
6. d
7. b
8. e

EXERCISE 2

1. D
2. F
3. J
4. H
5. I
6. B
7. G
8. C
9. A
10. E

EXERCISE 3

a. aspired
b. interred
c. exhuming
d. mountebanks
e. paramount
f. rustic
g. pastoral
h. promontories
i. terra cotta
j. ether

LESSON 11

EXERCISE 11A
1. d
2. d
3. c
4. e
5. e
6. a
7. d
8. e
9. b
10. a
11. b
12. d

EXERCISE 11B
1. d
2. b
3. c
4. c
5. b
6. c
7. d

EXERCISE 11C
1. b
2. c
3. e
4. d
5. b
6. a

EXERCISE 11D
1. flagrant
2. scintilla
3. incendiary
4. incenses
5. conflagration
6. pyrotechnics

LESSON 12

EXERCISE 12A
1. a
2. e
3. b
4. b
5. a
6. d
7. e
8. a
9. c

EXERCISE 12B
1. c
2. b
3. a
4. d
5. a
6. d
7. c
8. b
9. b

EXERCISE 12C
1. pontiff
2. effluent
3. redounds
4. Hydrologists
5. undulation
6. nave
7. pontificate
8. redundant
9. confluence
10. cormorant
11. *hudor, mar, unda*
12. dehydration
13. nauseate

EXERCISE 12D
1. meeting or flowing together
2. change or flow
3. papacy or papal reign
4. swamped or flooded or overwhelmed or overcome

REVIEW EXERCISES FOR LESSONS 11 AND 12

EXERCISE 1
1. d
2. e

EXERCISE 2
1. B, G
2. F, A
3. E, J
4. H, C
5. I, D

EXERCISE 3
a. flagrant
b. conflagrations
c. flux
d. inundating
e. pontificate

a. redounded
b. pyrotechnics
c. flamboyant
d. nave
e. confluence

EXERCISE 4
1. flagrant
2. redundant
3. flamboyant
4. pontificating
5. fervid
6. nauseated
7. incensed
8. confluent
9. caustic
10. effervescent

LESSON 13

EXERCISE 13A
1. d
2. b
3. d
4. c
5. c
6. e
7. d
8. c
9. e
10. b
11. a

EXERCISE 13B
1. b
2. b
3. d
4. b
5. a
6. c
7. c
8. d
9. a

EXERCISE 13C
1. ordained
2. insubordination
3. apostle
4. epistolary
5. asterisk
6. inordinate
7. ordinances
8. cosmology
9. constellation
10. rectify

EXERCISE 13D
1. constellation
2. rectify
3. apostles
4. ordained
5. ordinances
6. stellar

LESSON 14

EXERCISE 14A
1. a
2. e
3. d
4. a
5. e
6. b
7. a
8. e
9. c
10. a
11. b

EXERCISE 14B
1. c
2. b
3. c
4. b
5. c
6. c
7. d
8. d

EXERCISE 14C
1. penultimate
2. transmutes
3. temerity
4. immutable
5. dispersed
6. temperance
7. imperturbable
8. Permutations
9. ultimatum or ultimata
10. perturb
11. temerarious

EXERCISE 14D
1. ultimatum
2. outré
3. aspersions
4. temerariously
5. temerity
6. penultimate
7. temper
8. transmuting
9. turbid
10. immutable
11. perturbs

REVIEW EXERCISES FOR LESSONS 13 AND 14

EXERCISE 1
1. c
2. d
3. b
4. a

EXERCISE 2
1. d
2. e
3. a
4. e
5. b
6. c
7. c
8. e
9. c
10. b

EXERCISE 3
a. ultimatums
b. ordained
c. outré
d. cosmopolite
e. epistolary
f. dispersed
g. apostle
h. turbid
i. inordinate
j. perturb
k. temerity

LESSON 15

EXERCISE 15A
1. a
2. e
3. c
4. b
5. e
6. d
7. e
8. c
9. b
10. d

EXERCISE 15B
1. c
2. b
3. a
4. b
5. d
6. d
7. b
8. c

EXERCISE 15C
1. sojourn
2. millennia or millenniums
3. anachronism
4. chronicle(s)
5. extempore or extemporaneous
6. nocturnal
7. synchronous or synchronized
8. diurnal
9. biennially
10. equinoxes
11. *Annals*
12. temporizing

EXERCISE 15D
1. millennia or millenniums
2. *Nocturne*
3. sojourn
4. anachronistic
5. extempore or extemporaneous
6. superannuation
7. synchronous
8. *Meridian*
9. biennially
10. temporize

LESSON 16

EXERCISE 16A
1. b
2. e
3. d
4. a
5. d
6. c
7. b
8. c
9. b
10. e
11. e
12. c
13. a
14. c
15. e

EXERCISE 16B
1. d
2. d
3. c
4. a

EXERCISE 16C
1. memorabilia
2. memoirs
3. duress
4. neoclassical
5. moratorium
6. nova
7. senescence
8. immemorial
9. surly or dour
10. obdurate or surly or dour
11. novice or neophyte

EXERCISE 16D
1. memorabilia
2. immemorial
3. obdurate
4. neophyte
5. novices
6. duress
7. dour
8. surly
9. obdurate
10. senescent

REVIEW EXERCISES FOR LESSONS 15 AND 16

EXERCISE 1
1. c
2. d
3. b
4. d
5. b
6. c
7. a

EXERCISE 2
1. E
2. G
3. J
4. C
5. L
6. A
7. F
8. K
9. B
10. D
11. H
12. I

EXERCISE 3
a. synchronous
b. demurred
c. duress
d. obdurately

a. novice
b. extempore
c. surly
d. sojourn
e. moratorium
f. annals